His Heart Changes Everything

HIS HEART CHANGES EVERYTHING

The Church in the Wilderness

COURTNEY REDELSHEIMER

Published by Among Us Publishing
A Division of Among Us Ministries
Plymouth, MN

> Among Us Publishing is a ministry within Among Us Ministries, a publishing group dedicated to the local church and the lost within our communities. We believe God's vision at Among Us is to lead men, women and children to seek their destinies in Christ in order to strengthen, empower and direct their faith into His will for their lives.
>
> We pray that this Among Us book will help you discover how deep His heart is for you and encourage you to see yourself as He does.
>
> *For more information and resources from Among Us Ministries, please call:* 763-220-2455, *email* amongusministries@gmail.com *or visit us at* www.amongusministries.org.

Printed in the U.S.A.
All Scripture quotations, unless otherwise noted, indicated, are taken from the Amplified Bible (AMP). Copyright 2015 by The Lockman Foundation. Used by permission. www.Lockman.org
Other versions used are:
NKJ – Scripture taken from the New King James Version. Copyright 1982 by Thomas Nelson, Inc. Used by permission. All rights reserved.
ONM – Scripture taken from The One New Man Bible, copyright 2011 William J. Murford. Used by permission of True Potential Publishing, Inc.
MSG – Scripture taken from The Message, Copyright 1993,1994,1995,1996,2000,2001,2002. Used by permission of NavPress Publishing Group.
Sarah Family Ministries mentioned in dedication page is a Christian Ministerial Training Center with the vision to equip the saints that they might fulfill the ministry which they have been given from the Lord. http://www.sarahfamilyministries.org
Hebrew Heritage Calendars referenced in Chapter Eight are available from The Galilee Calendar Company, an Israel-based marketplace ministry. Proceeds help support ministry and humanitarian works in the land of Israel. Contact at: (on the web) www.GalileeCalendarCompany.com (email) admin@GalileeCalendarCompany.com (telephone) U.S. - (local call rings in Israel) 718-514-7127 Israel - 972527372888
All references to deity have been capitalized by the author. All emphasis within Scripture quotations is the author's own.

Copyright ©2017 by Courtney Redelsheimer
All rights reserved

Cover design by Steve Plummer / SPBookDesign
Interior design by Steve Plummer / SPBookDesign
Edited by Delores Topliff, John Redelsheimer, Carol Grabrian
Interior Photos by Katie Tsampis, Rachel Kuelbs, and Victoria Davis
Interior Map of Wilderness by Nathan Grabrian

ISBN-10: 0-9984751-8-1
ISBN-13: 978-0-9984751-8-9

The Man Comes Around
Words and Music by John R Cash
Copyright © 2002 Song of Cash, Inc.
All Rights Administered by BMG Rights Management (US) LLC
All Rights Reserved Used by Permission
Reprinted by Permission of Hal Leonard LLC

To our Lord and Savior, Jesus Christ, thank you. I place this book on Your altar and pray it is as You would have it to be, a story of Your love for Your precious Church.

To my family, all of you, who hunger after all that Christ is and all we are in Him.

To my beloved husband and children, the family God chose for us has made all the difference.

To all His precious people at Sarah Family Ministries, thank you for the humble service you offer before our Lord in teaching, training, and equipping us for our journey.

CONTENTS

Map of the Wilderness 8
    Step One   How? 11
    Step Two   What Can We Expect on Our Journey? 31
    Chapter 1   Purely His 37
    Chapter 2   Truthfully His. 49
    Chapter 3   Peacefully His 67
    Chapter 4   Joyfully His 87
    Chapter 5   Wisely His. 97
    Chapter 6   Powerfully His 109
    Chapter 7   Mercifully His. 125
    Chapter 8   Completely His 147

THE CHURCH IN THE WILDERNESS

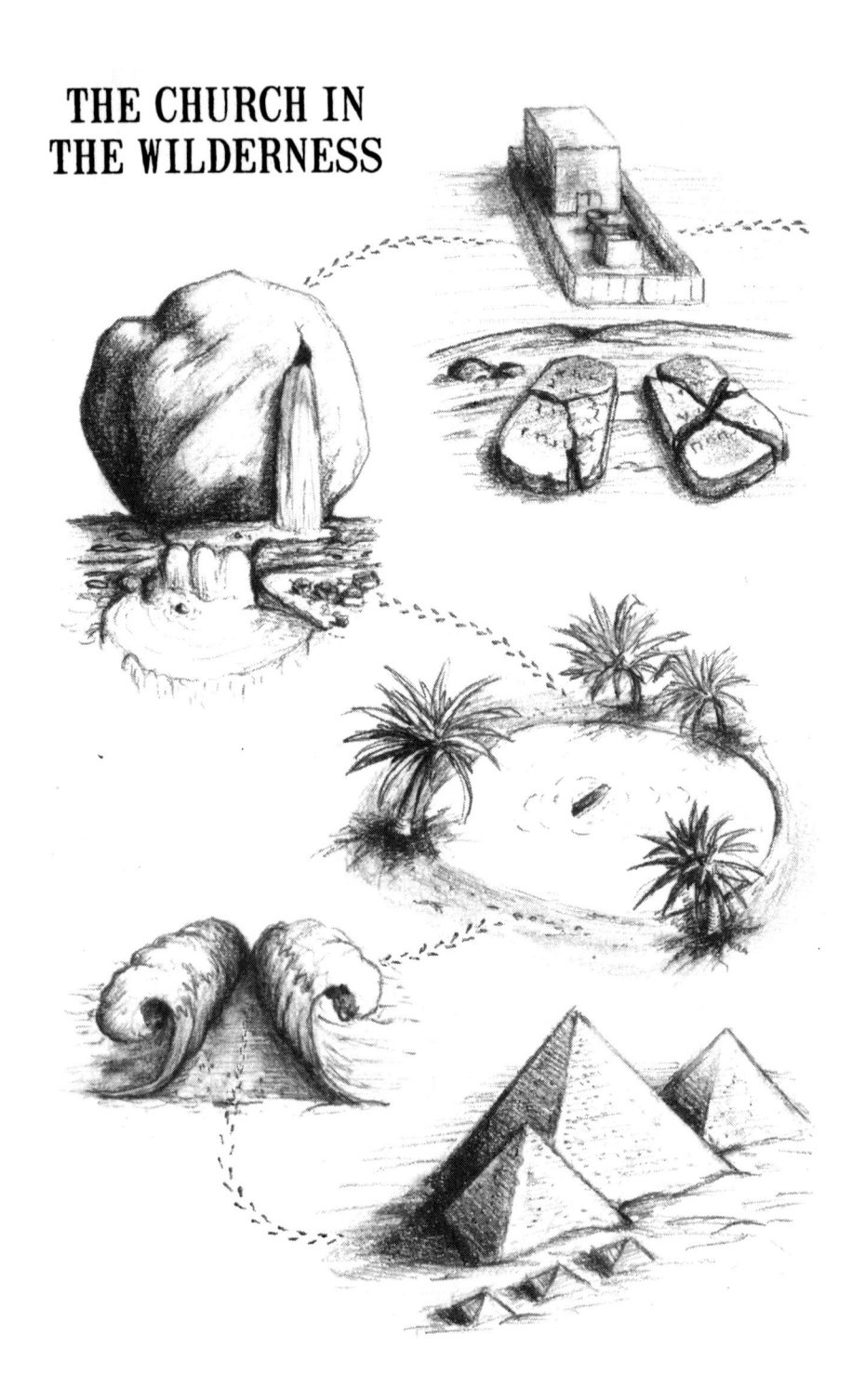

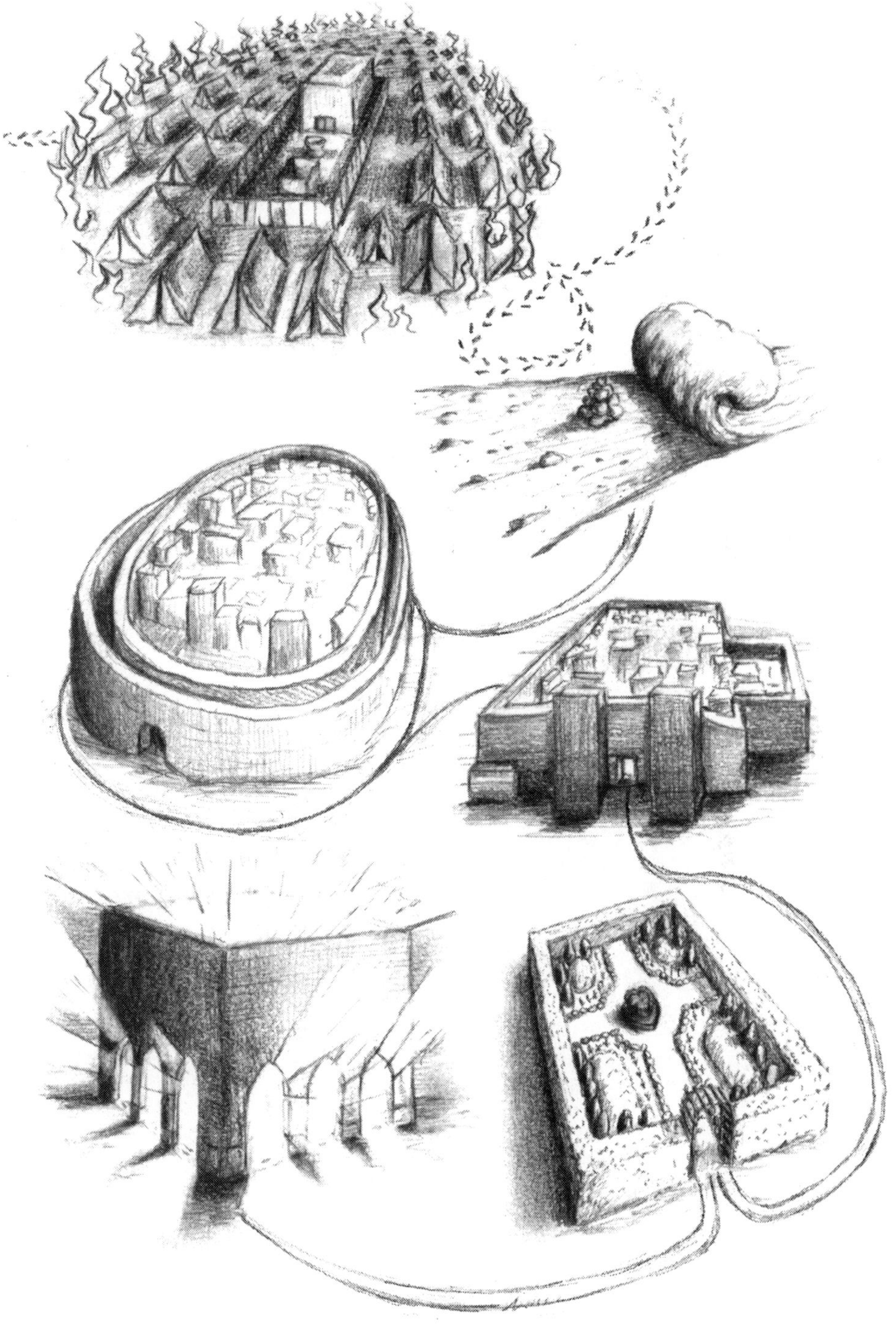

Step One

HOW?

ANSWER: GOD LURES US INTO THE WILDERNESS

I will take My children into the Wilderness and there I will speak tenderly to them. I will restore their fruitfulness and turn their valley of trouble into a door of hope.
(HOSEA 2:14-15)

JOSHUA COULD FEEL the slow and rhythmic beating of his heart in his chest as he waited for the agreed-upon sign from Moses. He looked out in front of him and knew that not far away the Amalekites were getting their troops ready to attack his men. The heat of the sun was already making the air above the rocks dance like smoke from a fire as it wiggled and wrapped its translucent fingers around their ankles and tickled the toes of their feet—these feet that had walked toward their freedom from Egypt just forty-three days ago following the rod of God in Moses' hand. The Israelites in their sandaled feet had walked on dry ground through the Red Sea and across the hot, dry, Wilderness of Sin. God had taken the dust of this desolate place and provided manna for food and water for drinking. While some were awed by this kind and loving God, many had grumbled and complained. Joshua had been amazed and humbled and now he waited with his handpicked troop of warriors. Some waited patiently, others anxiously, while Joshua kept his eyes on Moses waiting for the signal that would be the rod of God held high in Moses' hand—the first battle to keep their newborn freedom was about to begin.

Joshua had watched closely as his family learned to follow Moses in the wilderness. Each step they took deepened his trust of God. This day, as he found himself leading his regiment of God's people, his heart moved into that deep trusting refuge of his and God's relationship. He knew that God was with them and that if they obeyed, the Lord would fight this battle for them. The Lord had become Joshua's banner; it was His glory that Joshua was thinking about in this moment, not his own or his family's. It was for the Lord that he would fight and lead and win this day and all others. Joshua watched as Moses' arms were raised up above his head. In his hand was the rod of God, which Moses now lifted high into the yellow sky. It was the sign for which Joshua had been waiting. Joshua turned to his troops to give them one last prayer of encouragement then turned back to face the enemy. With faith grown in the trials of God's wilderness, Israel began the march forward.

In an entirely different time and place, my daughter was facing the first steps into God's new course for her life. Her simple white wedding gown lay perfectly still against her legs in the heat of a smothering July afternoon. She lingered under the arbor of flowers as she waited for the minister's signal to take her first steps forward to meet her bridegroom. She could see him at the front of the crowd waiting for her with a peaceful joy she had come to know and love so deeply. He was so handsome in his full Marine dress and his white cap, which was perched perfectly straight on top of his head. The lid of the cap almost hid his bright blue eyes but it couldn't hide the wide grin that flashed at us from beneath its shadow.

By the time our daughter took her first few steps down the aisle, I felt ready to burst. I was so full of joy that by the time my youngest son stepped into his role as the ring bearer, I was beginning to tear up. This disarming little four-year-old, dressed in his tuxedo and holding the wedding rings in his hands, walked carefully toward the altar. The best man, another tall Marine in full uniform, proceeded to get down on one knee in front of my little boy. My son stood there for a minute looking up at him, then carefully handed over the rings. Satisfied that his job was accomplished, he turned his face back to me and scrambled into my lap.

We who have asked Jesus to be the Lord of our lives are like His bride waiting patiently and expectantly under the arbor of His love. Jesus, our bridegroom, came to be not only our Savior but the Savior of the world. He paid a bride price in his death and resurrection for our sins. He invites us to accept that price and become His bride. In Him and only in Him we are made right with God. He is now seated at the right hand of the Father, making a place for us and waiting for the signal from the Father that it is time to come bring us home.

The acceptance of His price and our *yes* to His invitation are just the beginning of our relationship with Jesus. He wants more than just our outward 'yes,' He wants our ALL. A bride knows her groom a little when they get engaged and will get to know him much more as they plan the wedding. When we say *yes* to Jesus becoming our groom we know Him a little. He wants us to know Him as He knows us. He wants us to grow to love Him with all our heart, mind, soul and strength. That kind of love will change our hearts and our lives.

In our culture today, we often follow up the wedding with a honeymoon. It was on this type of journey that my own marriage was first tested. A hurricane developed while we were on a cruise in the Atlantic Ocean. As the ship tipped to its side and 'all hands on deck' was called over the loud speakers we were all given raw glimpses into each other's hearts. In a similar fashion, Jesus will lure His new bride into the wilderness. He wants to be alone with us, far from familiar people and away from secure sights and sounds. These wilderness journeys are where He begins to introduce Himself as our Lord and Savior. His intent in these unfamiliar places is to awe us, prepare us, and discipline us to know Him as He already knows us. These are the places where we grow our faith in Him that in turn leads us to even deeper wilderness journeys and deeper faith. His love for us is like a precious, spiritual oil that enters us as we obey and walk in His ways, following His rod into whatever place He leads us. As we trust Him to provide and protect, we open ourselves wider to the flow of oil, which can be lit into a fire that burns bright for all to see. We, His children, become human lamps to light up His truth and guide others in His way. The light of our lamps reveals His banner of love over our lives. It is His banner of love that will lead others home to Him.

This banner of love is first woven for us as we begin to realize that He first loved us. Even when we were steeped in our own troubles, with no hope of getting out, God sent His only Son to die for our sins that we might be free to love. This was His plan from the beginning; before we had breath, He knew us and planned us perfectly. Joshua was under this banner when he marched into battle against the enemies of God, the Amalekites. I clung to this banner as I watched our children on their wedding day. I knew they were about to be tested because this is God's way of revealing what is in our hearts. We often think of our hearts as dependable. We picture them as pure and smooth like white sand until God takes the sifter out and we discover there are other things mixed in there—some good and some bad. God wants our hearts to be full of love and He is love. Anything in our hearts that wasn't put there by Him can be removed which gives our hearts more room for His pure love. Just like a dirty sandbox can be cleaned, so our hearts can be cleaned. The first step is to decide what banner we will carry, God's or the world's? His banner over us is His love, which is grown in us as we cling to Him through the sifting of trials and suffering.

Step 1: How?

God's design for His people is for good and to give them abundant life. It is the ungodly things in our hearts and our lives that separate us from the fullness of His promises. We tend to resist the changes He impresses on us and so He allows us to go to a place where we can see what He sees and desire what He desires. This place is called the wilderness and it is for sifting our hearts and redirecting our steps onto His path in order to follow His way.

The wilderness takes on many different forms depending on our hearts and character, but in each case it is God who lures us out there and it is us who either say 'yes' or 'no' to the trip. Jacob and Esau were the twin grandsons of Abraham. Jacob, the younger of the two, tricked his nearly blind father Isaac into giving him the older son's blessing that rightfully belonged to Esau. This trick ultimately led Jacob to flee into the wilderness to avoid Esau's anger. In the wilderness Jacob's heart and character were disciplined and matured until he became a man who would trust and obey God. Joshua followed Moses into the wilderness expecting to live in the Promised Land, then led the doubting Israelites back into the wilderness as they faced God's judgment. John the Baptist spent his whole ministry in the wilderness preaching repentance in preparation for a Savior who would baptize him. Instead, John the Baptist found himself baptizing the Savior. Jesus chose to go into the wilderness, knew what to expect, and came out in power. Saul, expecting to persecute Christians was thrown from his horse on the wilderness-road to Damascus where Jesus took his sight and his name and changed them to be His Paul. What does God have for you there?

Expectations can be tricky for all of us. As I watched the minister speak the vows over these precious children of God, I recalled our daughter's first steps in life. She had been an early talker and walker, always seeming to be a few months ahead of all baby book expectations. I decided early on in this, my first child's life, to try and stay alert. I determined to always be a few feet in front of her so I could lay a path that would be clear for her to follow. I didn't know it at the time, but our life together was not going to be anything like what I was expecting and planning. God had another plan for us and it would be so abundantly better. Never would I have expected the plan that He knew we must follow. It was so radically different than my hopes that it took me by surprise and shook my world. This is what changes our hearts in the wilderness. When our expectations come face to face with the King of the Universe and we say 'yes' to His and relinquish ours. This is how we begin to allow His banner to come over us as we learn to walk in His way. Jesus tells a parable about a man who chose to say 'no' and thought he would do things his own way instead of the king's way. In the story, the king prepares a great banquet for his son's wedding and sends out his servants to summon the people who have been invited to the feast. The first group of people who are invited ignore the invitation and don't come. The king tries again to convince the people to come and they still ignore his summons. Some of these people go so far as to kill the king's messengers and this makes the king extremely angry. He sends his troops to kill those murderers and burn their city. Finally the king declares those invited to be unworthy and sends his servants into the main roads to invite as many people as they find. According to custom of the day the servants would have given each guest a particular wedding garment to be worn in the banquet hall. All the guests would have been expected to be dressed according to the king's garment. According to Jesus' story, when the king enters the wedding banquet and is carefully examining all of his guests he is alarmed to see one man who does not have on the expected garment (Matthew 22). The parable does not tell us why this man was dressed wrongly, only what happened to him because of it. The man may have believed his own clothes to be good enough and so refused the covering offered by the king. The truth is, God wants us to be rightly clothed and He has provided the way for us to be clothed in His righteousness. It is the only way we will enter the wedding feast with our Savior, His Son, Jesus Christ. I personally, don't want to miss it.

> *I will greatly rejoice in the Lord, my soul will exult in my God; for He has clothed me with the garments of salvation, He has covered me with the robe of righteousness, as a bridegroom decks himself with a garland, and as a bride adorns herself with her jewels (Isaiah 61:10).*

The garment Isaiah was prophesying about has been provided to those who are called/invited to the Kings (God's) wedding banquet. That garment is Jesus Christ, our Messiah. Those who believe they can work out their own righteousness apart from Christ are going to find themselves in a similar circumstance to the man in the wedding banquet who refused to put on the king's wedding garment.

> *And He said, Friend, how did you come in here without putting on the appropriate wedding garment? And he was speechless (muzzled, gagged). Then the king said to the attendants, tie him hand and foot, and throw him into the darkness outside; there will be weeping and grinding of teeth. For many are called (invited and summoned), but few are chosen. (Matthew 22: 12-14)*

I very much want to be dressed correctly for God when He puts on the wedding feast for His Son, Jesus Christ. When we answer 'yes' we begin to learn how to put His garment on. His Spirit, which is Jesus in us, begins to train us in His way of doing things. We begin to learn to hear Him, and obey Him. Little by little, we learn to take our first steps. Then we learn to walk, run, march, skip and even do hurdles in our new clothes of Christ. The Israelites had a similar choice to make when they approached the Promised Land for the first time and God's truth didn't match their expectations. The 'giants' in the land surprised and overwhelmed them. They doubted God and decided to say 'no.' Why did this happen? What did the Promised Land mean to the Israelites? Did they have the whole picture of how God's promises would look? What were they expecting? What do we desire right now in our present lives, for our hearts, our relationships, and our homes? Are we about to enter the wilderness? Have we come up to the 'Promised Land' only to find it didn't meet our expectations and scared us away? Or are we like Joshua or like Caleb: ready for the promise and trained in how to enter, fight for, and keep the faith? Do we have His banner over us?

I came to know Jesus' way of doing things by first failing miserably in my attempts to do things my own way. I knew that I wanted marriage because I wanted to love and be loved. I knew these desires were good things, so I set about getting them. I was successful in my efforts, and at the age of twenty-four I found myself married. Four years later I had my first child, a daughter. I also discovered very quickly that I had no idea what I was doing. Intense emotional and dramatic conflict seemed to escalate uncontrollably after the birth of my daughter. I found myself trying to de-escalate these events by relying on my own understanding. My own understanding would prove to be fatally flawed.

Somewhere in my life I had become convinced that to be successful in any relational conflict a person could do one of two things: The first option was to allow my emotions to be known, clearly, strongly, and honestly or; option two, which was my preference, if possible, avoid conflict entirely. My favorite means of avoiding conflict was to try to fix everything—in other words, to be perfect for everyone. I soon found out that marriage could not run on either of these two choices. I was faced with the only other thing I knew how to do: separate off, box up what I was feeling, and move on. I was thirty-one years old and my little girl was three when we left our home and entered a women's shelter. That was Palm Sunday, 1998.

> *Lean on, trust in, and be confident in the Lord with all your heart and mind and do not rely on your own insight or understanding. In*

> all your ways know, recognize, and acknowledge Him, and He will direct and make straight and plain your paths. Be not wise in your own eyes; reverently fear and worship the Lord and turn [entirely] away from evil. (Proverbs 3:5-7)

I heard Jesus call my name that same year, I said 'yes' and He immediately set about the work of changing my heart so I would walk on His path. He did this by luring me into the unavoidable wilderness journey of growing up. Somehow at thirty-one years old I had managed to stay a child who didn't really know who I was supposed to be unless someone told me. We can choose to do things the hard way or the easy way. I had spent much of my life in quiet, and sometimes not so quiet, rebellion against those in authority—first my parents, then my husband. The rebellion I chose wasn't the normal kind. My wounds weren't obvious and direct or easily definable. I had grown to be an adult that was accustomed to the power of rejection and harbored a constant expectation of abandonment. Wounds caused by not getting our needs met are often hidden behind quiet thoughts of confusion and self-hatred. Now, in the love of Christ, I would begin the lesson of submitting to authority, godly or not and in the process I would learn what it means to be loved by God.

> THE LORD is my Shepherd [to feed, guide, and shield me], I shall not lack. (Psalm 23:1)

I didn't know much about Jesus when I began my journey, but as I struggled through divorce and custody battles, I came to understand His grace and provision for all of us. It would be a two-year conflict through some of the most difficult and unexpected trials of my life. I could not let my emotions take over, and I had to try be as good a mother as I could even as my three-year-old was facing new and unknown experiences of her own. I had to submit to the law and lawyers and be a bridge of communication and respect with my now ex-husband and his soon-to-be new wife.

A friend of mine told me a wonderful story about her son and kindergarten that will illustrate my mindset at that time. Her little boy was a tender and sensitive child. Knowing his disposition, she had spent months carefully preparing her son so he would be ready for his first day of school. When the big day finally arrived, mother and son met the bus together. The little boy marched right onto the bus and sat down, no problem at all. In the afternoon, the bus pulled up to the corner, the little boy got off just brimming with excitement, and ran up to his mother shouting with glee: "Phew, Mom, I sure am glad that's over with!" My friend had failed to make it clear to her relieved child that the first day of school was only the first of many.

When the divorce proceedings, courtroom dramas, and all that accompanied it was at last over, I had much the same reaction. "Phew, Praise God, that's over with!" I was not prepared for the emotional, mental undertow that inevitably grabs those who are unaware. The devil's plan to kill, steal, and destroy is constant, and if we rest when God is not, we can be snared (John 10:10). I thought when the divorce ended I was done. I had passed the test and could begin to put our lives back together in a restful and conflict-free home. I truly believed I was ready to enter the 'promised land.' I did not have a clue how much more Jesus had planned for us or how much more of Him I needed in my heart.

There were some major missing pieces in the puzzle of living for Christ. First of all, I was not born again and had only just started attending church. I was still largely untrained and ill-prepared for the responsibilities and maturity required to take on that into which our lives would lead us. Secondly, I thought I needed to be all grown up *now*. I had been granted custody, and as head of our household—I thought— I would need to work very hard. Here was the biggest issue of all, I thought Jesus had gotten me to this point and that I was expected to be thankful (which I was) and that I should take it from there. Let me repeat what I just said there, because this would be a snare for me more than once and I believe it is a snare for others:

> *I thought that Jesus had gotten me to a certain point and that I WAS SUPPOSED TO TAKE IT FROM THERE. That was a lie from Satan. The fact that I believed it meant I really did not know Jesus yet at all.*

I believe this same limited understanding of 'who Jesus is' keeps many of us from reaching our fullness in Christ's plan for our lives. We look forward to His rest, which He does give, but then we can get stuck there. Thinking we have reached the summit of the mountain, we sit back to enjoy the view. We don't realize that there is another summit to climb and many more lessons to learn. It seems He has created in us an endless tapestry of color and gifting that can only come forth in the stretching and pulling of trials and suffering walked through in faith.

Faith means trusting in Christ for what we need and being accountable for the faith we say we have. He delivers us through faith from the corruption that is in the world because of sin so that we may become partakers in His nature (2Peter 1:2-4). As we put His gifts into action through faith and allow His divine nature to be the controller of our lives, we become lamps filled with His light and love. We rest, but must always keep an eye out for when He moves. Movements of God mean opportunities to train. As Abraham obeyed by faith when God said "go" so we too are expected to be actively involved in our personal growth as Christians. When God gets up and starts up that next hill, we need to be close by His side, trusting and anticipating what the next journey will reveal of our hearts.

> *For this very reason, adding your diligence [to the divine promises], employ every effort in exercising your faith to develop virtue (excellence, resolution, Christian energy), and in [exercising] virtue [develop] knowledge (intelligence), And in [exercising] knowledge*

> [develop] self-control, and in [exercising] self-control [develop] steadfastness (patience, endurance), and in [exercising] steadfastness [develop] godliness (piety), And in [exercising] godliness [develop] brotherly affection, and in [exercising] brotherly affection [develop] Christian love. For as these qualities are yours and increasingly abound in you, they will keep [you] from being idle or unfruitful unto the [full personal] knowledge of our Lord Jesus Christ (the Messiah, the Anointed One). For whoever lacks these qualities is blind, [spiritually] shortsighted, seeing only what is near to him, and has become oblivious [to the fact] that he was cleansed from his old sins. Because of this, brethren, be all the more solicitous and eager to make sure (to ratify, to strengthen, to make steadfast) your calling and election; for if you do this, you will never stumble or fall. Thus there will be richly and abundantly provided for you entry into the eternal kingdom of our Lord and Savior Jesus Christ. (2Peter 1: 5-11)

As the Israelites came out of the wilderness from their last walk across the Sinai, freedom in the Promised Land may have held an expectation of ease and rest from their enemies. Each tribe sent in one scout to see if their expectations were real. I imagine that as they set out on their journey into the land, each one had already spent considerable time dreaming of what they hoped to see. Perhaps one of them wanted the highlands with fanciful ideas of mountains full of spices and scenic views. Maybe another imagined valleys with peaceful rivers and lush vegetation. In our eras vocabulary; one person wanted a penthouse with a view, and the other wanted a riverside cabin for a fishing retreat. Clearly, most of the Israelites were not expecting to see antagonistic, unfriendly, giant people living in *their Promised Land* behind giant and seemingly insurmountable stonewalls. This could NOT be what God had in mind! Could it?

Some of us have very definite desires for our lives. I have come to call these our core convictions. These are places in our hearts around which we have built a strong castle on a foundation of our own expectations. We surround this mental/emotional fortress with walls and a moat to protect our desires, and then we close the door. These conviction castles can be godly or they can be ungodly but they will not stand long if they are both. Godly castles are based on God's desires for us and His people and draw others to see Him and His holiness. They are built on the development of the awe of God in our hearts and the exercising of His character in our lives. In other words, they are built on the rock, which is Christ.

Ungodly castles are founded on our own personal fears, emotions and desires. They focus everyone on us, our needs, and magnify our strengths. These castles are built on the awe of people in our hearts and our hope to impress or control them. This fear of people and what they can or can't do for us or to us controls our heart and our actions. These castles are built on sand (Matt 7:24-26).

Our hearts choose which castle to build based on our experiences, learning, and expectations. We must have one or the other, we cannot have castles or walls built on both sand and rock and expect them to stay standing for very long. The first storm that comes along will wash away the sand. Trying to mix awe of God with fear of man will build a weak castle that eventually requires full renovation. We cannot serve two masters, and a house divided will fall (Matthew 6:24, Mark 3:25).

After the divorce, I developed strong core convictions about love. I was much wounded and hoped desperately to find comfort in God's Word. I read about a man's command to love his wife and a wife's command to respect her husband. I began to build my new castle that would be based on the perfect marriage and family. I had the Word right but I wasn't mixing the Word with faith in God. I was mixing the Word with faith in myself and some other imagined man with whom I would complete this perfect castle. In the splintering of my first marriage I was supposed to have seen that it wasn't simply the people in my marriage that were at issue, the problem lay in both of our hearts.

Our hearts as human beings are deceitful (Jeremiah 17:9) and even if they have been born again in Christ and are holding new, clean materials and tools for God's extreme makeover, any structure they build will continue to be unreliable until they come to rest completely on the foundational rock of Christ. My heart, in its natural passion to build began to construct a castle full of love, respect, safety, good teaching and sound discipline. I followed my heart (isn't that what the world is always saying to do) and built this thing myself with the Word of God mixed with my own understanding and willpower. My faith in myself and my own desire to love and be loved was the foundation. I walled this conviction castle, built a moat around it, closed the door tight and waited. I was going to hang tough until some man came along that proved worthy of me opening the door and lowering the draw bridge.

The prince charming I hoped for arrived in 2002 and I lowered the drawbridge. He entered my castle and joined it with his own castle full of his convictions, his own moat, and added a horse stable full of unbroken, frisky, wild stallions that were his friends and family members. We were married in the spring of 2003. I had been living alone with my daughter for five years and I embraced our new life and our new family with gusto. Our home now included two sons, aged nine and five, my daughter, age eight, a turtle named Spike, a dog named Harvey, and two cats, Charlie and Fitch.

Jesus almost immediately began to work on dismantling our castles. We did not realize we even had them, but God knew that to survive, our new life had to be built on the rock of Jesus alone. Everything built on the sand or the rock and sand had to come down. Little by little, stone by stone, over the course of twelve years Jesus took the walls of our personal expectations down. We found ourselves facing year thirteen of marriage staring at two destroyed castles and one square slab of cracked cement precariously perched between sand and rock. This foundation represented our now broken hearts where lies, emotional conflict, and unmet expectations had proved to be just what Jesus promised—a house built on sand. The rain had come down, just like He promised, and the floods came up, just like He said they would, and the house built on sand went splat (Matthew 7:24-27).

We looked like what I might imagine Israel looked like to Ezra and Nehemiah when they returned to Jerusalem after the Babylonian destruction of the city in 586 BC. They came to take part in the rebuilding of God's temple, the peoples' houses, and eventually the walls of the city. My husband and I were faced with essentially the same daunting task. Our marriage needed to be rebuilt but this time on Him and Him alone. Thankfully, only by the grace of God, we were both excited for this restoration project.

When we've been broken and humbled, the world around us can seem gigantic and scary. It's a place where we can fall into fear of man, but His hope is that we will instead discover the awe of God (Numbers 14:6-9). As my husband and I stood at this juncture, God asked us a simple question, "What do you want?" We both answered that we wanted to try again, and in His mercy God granted us that longing. We wanted the banner over us, this time, to be His love, not our own.

The Israelites who were delivered from slavery in Egypt to follow God to the Promised Land were also humbled, broken, and vulnerable. We don't know for sure what they were expecting in the Promised Land, but whatever it was, ten of them didn't see the promise and instead saw the giants (Numbers 13). Ten of their hearts hadn't grown to trust God enough to embrace His promised land because the giants were unexpected but they were also familiar. The fear of Egypt and the oppression there overwhelmed their faith in God's promise and they lost hope. There were only two spies who brought good reports full of faith and courage. Two who had allowed their hearts to embrace the justice and holiness of the rod of God in the wilderness. These two trusted that He would win the battle against the giants because it was His banner they served (Numbers 14:24).

Which will we be when He brings us to His promised land? God, please let us be like Joshua and Caleb. Let our wilderness journeys prepare our hearts for YOUR plan and purpose, not for our own imagined schemes. Let our hearts be sanctified in order that we will love Your people like You love them and in the way that You would have us love them. Lord Jesus we pray that we will stop fearing men and we will start believing You. Lord, help us with our unbelief (Mark 9:24)!

> *Having purified your souls by your obedience to the truth for a sincere brotherly love, love one another earnestly from a pure heart.* (1 Peter 1:22)

Bad reports come from our fears. Understandably, the Israelites were afraid of being oppressed and enslaved again by the giants they heard reported were living in the land. The giants were real; the spies weren't telling lies, but they failed to take the truth of the giants back to God for His instruction. They believed what they saw with their natural eyes and understood with their minds separated from what they should have understood of God. They had just experienced such amazing things with Him in the wilderness, yet they didn't mix those miraculous experiences with what they were now seeing. God wants us to learn to believe what we don't see—to live by faith and trust in Him instead of trusting in what is familiar to our understanding.

I know how those Israelites felt. I had a keen sense of what had caused me pain in the past, and I was unwilling to get wounded again. Like being kicked in the shins by a toddler, you learn to stay clear. I was willing to stay clear of marriage the rest of my life. Once I was brave enough to get married again, I thought I should avoid having more children. What if there was another divorce? I was afraid to quit work and step out into ministry. What if I couldn't support myself and there was another divorce? These thoughts are the whispering voices of our enemy who loves to feed on our fears. If we allow distrust and doubt to ask us the questions of "What if?"

without answering back in faith then we will allow our enemy to begin to create bitter fruit in our hearts. If we enter into these conversations and agree with the voice of the enemy, then we will stay in our own castles and build our own walls and moats and keep our doors closed. We will also have lots of company because we will have and attract friends that share all our same fears. Locked inside with all this familiarity and agreement we won't ever have to go out or grow up because no one will make us face our fears—until the rain comes, and it will come.

What are the things that can cause you to get defensive or angry? If there is fear in your heart, the opportunity exists for the devil to make that fear become a giant in your land. For example, we might worry that we aren't lovable or that we aren't needed. That can turn the reality of being alone, unmarried, unemployed, or childless into a perceived giant in our land. If we don't turn to Jesus with this fear and learn what He says about being alone, unmarried, unemployed, or childless, then we will create our own answers. We could decide in our deceitful hearts that marriage, children, or busyness is the answer to our fears. If we are convinced enough, we can pursue our own answers to such a degree that they replace Jesus in our lives. When something replaces or overwhelms Jesus, it is now an idol. Idols compete for His presence in our hearts. The devil then begins to have a hold on us in these areas and his goal is to add on to these idols until they all merge into one large forbearing structure that we are sure we can never live safely without.

> *We can pursue our own answers to such a degree that they replace Jesus in our lives.*

These strongholds of idols are formed in sin, and unrepented sin separates us from God. Keeping our hands tightly wrapped around people in order to control their ability to hurt us can tempt us to build strongholds around these fears. Keeping our parents and children safely tucked inside its thick and seemingly secure walls will make it look like we have succeeded in securing our lives. Any security found in human efforts is motivated by the devil's lies and is destined to prove fruitless for God's kingdom. These false securities take our focus off of God's ability and puts our trust in self—until the rains come, and they will.

God allows trials so that we have the opportunity to see these idols and destroy them ourselves. His desire is to work in us a deeper and truer faith in Him. He wants these storms to teach us patience and steadfastness as we wait on Him and look for Him. He wants our patience to be tested so much that we become complete and lack nothing in Him (James 1:1-5). If we allow these godly trials to build our castle of self-protection, it will have proven our lack of faith. The fear we have will work its way into becoming an idol, and an idol's job is to compete with God for our thoughts and our focus, and most importantly, our love and obedience. If, on the other hand, we allow godly trials to have their whole work in us, we will allow God to reveal the idols in our hearts and will trust Him to take them and make us new. He will build us up on His rock as we become increasingly dependent on Him and increasingly distrustful of ourselves.

There is NOTHING our God cannot do! NOTHING. Persevering in prayer, in His will, and trusting in faith for the hope of His promises will destroy idols and replace them with His peace. Consistently turning our eyes toward Him and His truth will keep our foundation securely in/on Him. He promises there is perfect peace when our eyes are securely fixed on Him (Isaiah 26:3).

I don't want to be one of the ten Israelite spies with bad reports when I approach the 'promised land'. How about you? I want to be one of the two that is His remnant, represented here by Joshua and Caleb. They had faith and were hungry for the Lord and had learned to cling to the Lord with all their might. I want to be found with my eyes and hope totally set on Him. The 'remnant of two' had the faith and hope to stand and wait on Him and His plan no matter the circumstances that surrounded them because their hope was built on the rock of God, not the sand and not a mixture of rock and sand. I want to help others as they become a Joshua or a Caleb who are journeying through the wilderness of God, learning to fight the good fight and run the race under His banner of Love.

This book hopes to share with you the revelation of the love to be found in the wilderness of God. May He speak tenderly and softly as He leads you in the building of your heart on His Rock. He is always working for your good and for the good of your family (Deuteronomy 8:16 NASB). His goal and His earnest desire is to have your whole heart. We are His bride and He is preparing us to enter into the promise of His kingdom. Be patient and keep marching, because it can take a while. It took the Israelites seventy years to receive the promise that many of us cling to in Jeremiah 29:11

> *For thus says the Lord, when seventy years are completed for Babylon, I will visit you and keep My good promise to you, causing you to return to this place. For I know the thoughts and plans that I have for you, says the Lord, thoughts and plans for welfare and peace and not for evil, to give you hope in your final outcome. Then you will call upon Me, and you will come and pray to Me, and I will hear and heed you. Then you will seek Me, inquire for, and require Me [as a vital necessity] and find Me when you search for Me with all your heart. I will be found by you, says the Lord, and I will release you from captivity and gather you from all the nations and all the places to which I have driven you, says the Lord, and I will bring you back to the place from which I caused you to be carried away captive. (Jeremiah 29:10-14)*

As my daughter turned around with her husband, they took a moment to breathe in the scene in front of them. There, like a sea of love, sat all their family and close friends. What a great gift we have in Jesus. In Him, love bears all things, believes all things, and unifies all people, bringing down their castles of self and connecting them with bridges of understanding and shared focus in Christ (1Corinthians 13).

If I give everything I own to the poor and even go to the stake to be burned as a martyr, but I don't love, I've gotten nowhere. So, no matter what I say, what I believe, and what I do, I'm bankrupt without love. Love never gives up. Love cares more for others than for self. Love doesn't want what it doesn't have. Love doesn't strut, Doesn't have a swelled head, Doesn't force itself on others, Isn't always "me first," Doesn't fly off the handle, Doesn't keep score of the sins of others, Doesn't revel when others grovel, Takes pleasure in the flowering of truth, Puts up with anything, Trusts God always, Always looks for the best, Never looks back, But keeps going to the end. Love never dies. Inspired speech will be over some day; praying in tongues will end; understanding will reach its limit. We know only a portion of the truth, and what we say about God is always incomplete. But when the Complete arrives, our incompletes will be canceled

(1 Corinthians 13:3-10, The Message).

Step Two:

WHAT CAN WE EXPECT ON OUR JOURNEY?
ANSWER: THAT WE WILL SEE THE AWESOMENESS OF GOD!

So now finish doing it, that your [enthusiastic] readiness in desiring it may be equaled by your completion of it according to your ability and means
(2 CORINTHIANS 8:11).

OUR SON WAS reading "Paddle to the Sea" by Holling C. Holling during the time that I was writing this book. The book by Holling follows the travels of a hand carved canoe as it is launched from its home in the northern banks of Lake Nipigon, Canada and follows the rivers south into the currents of the Great Lakes and eventually out to the Atlantic Ocean. When we finished reading the book, John Jr. (our son) felt strongly that God was asking him to whittle his own canoe, paint it, carve a message into its side, pray over it and then set it free in Lake Nipigon, which is located in Ontario, Canada, about ten hours north of our home in Minnesota. He asked his dad to join him and John Senior prayed and agreed that he was to work alongside John Jr. as an encourager. His goal was to help his son complete this assignment from God. They both embraced in faith the job of designing, whittling and making buoyant, their own small wooden canoes.

On July 24, 2016, about six months from the time whittling began, two boats were launched into the waters of Nipigon River, Ontario. One was named Light Spreader and the other beside it was named Love. The day of the launch was dark and rainy from Thunder Bay to the city of Nipigon. We had ventured from the town itself up the Nipigon River to Lake Nipigon only to discover that the wind was whipping the currents toward the shore so roughly that the little boats would have been destroyed by the rocks. We prayed and consulted each other and finally decided that we would dip the boats here in the waters of Lake Nipigon but then drive south again along the Nipigon River and allow the Holy Spirit to lead us to a safer launching spot.

As we climbed out on the rocks of Lake Nipigon, and John Jr. gingerly placed his Light Spreader in the cold waters, the clouds parted and the sun came out bright and hot. It was amazing and instant. In our excitement we became distracted and failed to notice we had left both boats sitting on a park bench next to the lake. We were pulling out of the park when I thought to ask if everyone had their boats. After a hurried inspection of the vehicle we determined we must have left them back by the water. We turned the car around and headed back the way we had just come, hearts beating a little harder than usual and thoughts wondering about what we might expect to find.

As John Jr. walked out to the point where we had dipped the boats in the lake, he could see both the Light Spreader and Love sitting among a group of adults and children. They were excited and talking to each other as they turned the little boats around in their hands. As he approached he could hear that they were deciding what they should do with their discovery and unexpected responsibility. On the bottom of both canoes, John Jr. and his father had burned in the words *"Put me back in the water"* and this adopted family had attempted to obey. They too had discovered what we had, that the same wind was still threatening to push the boats back up against the rocks, hindering any possibility of their making it out into the lake to begin their journeys to the sea. A man who appeared to be the grandfather of the group had just suggested they wait a few hours to see if the wind changed when John Jr. approached to reclaim the boats. Already these two boats of faith had touched others as our son proceeded to share with the group the story of God's direction for these two brightly painted canoes.

Relieved to be back on the road, we took the boats and traveled down toward the river and Lake Superior. All the while, we were looking and listening for His Spirit to indicate where the final launch would be. We wondered if it would be in the Nipigon River or closer to where the river opened up into the bay of Lake Superior. As we drove, the weather again became cloudy and rainy and even windier than it had been earlier in the day.

We drove for more than an hour along the east side of Nipigon River, stopping to investigate a few places where we thought perhaps the Spirit was leading us. We drove for hours more, past small towns, a few people and a couple of bears. Finally, we found a road that took us up the west side of Nipigon River past a dam. We were well into the forests of Canada. We crossed a little bridge over the river and John Jr. sensed this was the place. We all climbed out of the car and made our way back to this small bridge that connected the two banks of the river.

John Jr. was holding his canoe in his hand and looking out over the river. The sky loomed dark and there was a persistent drizzle. We stood quietly behind him waiting to see what he would do. His eleven year old heart seemed troubled and he turned to me and asked if it had ever been hard for me to let something or someone go. I thought of all the times I had let his sister go, first at three years old to her dad's house for visits, then off to college, and most recently to California to begin her new life with her husband. I assured him I had felt that tightness. Then he asked me a question. He asked, "What am I supposed to do with this feeling?" I answered by sharing what God had shared with me about my children. I told John Jr. "When we know its time, and God has called them, we have to let them go." I tried to assure him that he would feel a release of the tightness in his heart as he sought God's grace to let go of the little canoe that had grown so dear to him.

He turned back to the river, and he wound up his best baseball arm and chucked Light Spreader into the water far from his ability to go get her and pull her out. She was launched, this time for good. My husband followed up by aiming his canoe down into the water right beside his son's. The two boats began to make their way together around the edge of the river toward the bay. As soon as the Light Spreader settled into the river, the clouds broke and the sun came through gentle and warm. God's approval of the launch seemed to glow down right on the spot where the two boats lingered and swayed until they caught a little current and began to journey together into places we will never know but can pray about and imagine.

We climbed quietly into our car all occupied with our own thoughts and wonders from the day. Our son hid behind the ear plugs of his iPod for most of the rest of that evening as the accomplishment of a task set by God sunk into his young heart. I noticed as the tightness in his jaw softened. Soon it was replaced by peace and then by joy. The affirmation that God had given him began to be fully embraced. Sending these boats off on a journey we could not take with them had truly been God's will and we had gotten to be a small part of that plan. The woe in his heart began to be replaced by the WOW of God. That is exactly what a wilderness journey does for us. It replaces our woe with WOW of God.

Step 2: What Can We Expect on Our Journey?

He lures us there for our good and His glory and we choose to obey or not based largely on our love and faith in Him (John 14:21).

Perhaps you can relate to this. Perhaps you have stood in a church, at work, or in a marriage and realized that what it looks like on the outside is not what is going on inside. Perhaps you have desperately longed for truth in both places, along with love and life, healing and freedom, and peace. The task of accomplishing this kind of sincere truth in our lives seems overwhelming and out of our reach. Yet there are some who persist in crying out for this truth and in response He reaches down and assures us He will do it.

Are you one of those who have persisted in crying out and seeking His truth? He promises to answer. We are challenged to trust and obey and persevere in patient faith. He understands our human frailty and He wants us to learn to depend on Him to accomplish this task and then many more. The key is in drawing nearer and nearer to Him, to the truth of Him. In becoming one with Him, as He and the Father are one. That is how close He wants to be. He wants to be one with us and us with Him. He promises to be faithful to accomplish this as we trust Him to lead each of us on this journey of becoming truly and totally His.

There is only one way to find out what is on the other side of His wilderness journey for you: it is to get up and go. Go and keep going toward what you believe He is telling you to do. Abraham went, Joshua went, Moses went, and the question before us is; will we go?

What promises does He have for us in this journey? There are no promises about where He will lead you, how long it will take to travel through, or how many times we will be asked to go back into the wilderness. There are also no promises about what we will experience while we are there. A successful wilderness journey will be completely given over to Him in faith. The only promise we have, if we have asked Him to be Lord of our lives, is that He goes with us. His rod and His staff will comfort us (Psalm 23).

He wants to become our all in all. If leaving our house or family or friends or job behind is too much of a cost, we will not be able to make the journey. We must be willing to let go of it all. It is worth paying the highest cost we can imagine. After all, He already paid the ultimate cost. Isn't it worth every penny and every trial to gain the heart of Christ? His kingdom is worth it all.

> *Again the kingdom of heaven is like a man who is a dealer in search of fine and precious pearls, Who, on finding a single pearl of great price, went and sold all he had and bought it.* (Matthew 13:45-46)

Chapter 1

PURELY HIS

'But the wisdom from above is first pure, then peaceable, gentle, open to reason, full of mercy and good fruits, impartial and sincere'.
(James 3:17)

Autobiography in Five Short Chapters:

Chapter 1
I walk down the street.
There is a deep hole in the sidewalk.
I fall in
I am lost...I am hopeless.
It isn't my fault.
It takes forever to find a way out.

Chapter 2
I walk down the same street.
There is a deep hole in the sidewalk.
I pretend I don't see it.
I fall in again.

I can't believe I am in this same place.
But it isn't my fault.
It still takes a long time to get out.

Chapter 3
I walk down the same street.
There is a deep hole in the sidewalk.
I see it there.
I still fall in...it's a habit...but,
My eyes are open.
I know where I am.
It's my fault.
I get out immediately.

Chapter 4
I walk down the same street.
There is a deep hole in the sidewalk.
I walk around it.

Chapter 5
I walk down another street.

(*There's A Hole in My Sidewalk*. 1993 by Portia Nelson)

> *Thus says the Lord: Stand by the roads and look; and ask for the eternal paths, where the good, old way is; then walk in it, and you will find rest for your souls. But they said, "We will not walk in it"!*
> (Jeremiah 6:16)

*D*o you remember the 'good old days' stories told around the table at family gatherings? Grandpa or grandma or some other elderly relative would begin with something like; "I remember when – and end with "see kids, those were the good old days." It didn't take us long to realize that trapesing several miles in brutally cold, South Dakota blizzards through a bull pasture with your brothers was necessarily better. What they were saying to us kids was, "sometimes hard stuff done together is good." It was good for the heart and good for the character. My grandmothers would both tell you that their washing machine and dishwasher were really wonderful inventions. However, I know they would also remind us that there was something lost when those machines replaced time spent side-by-side scrubbing everything by hand.

Something has been lost too in many of today's modern Churches. People who call themselves Christian but are not loyal to God's Word and don't seek a deeper relationship with His Spirit are at risk of losing their connection to Jesus Christ. The spirit of the world that lures us to cooperate with worldly peace and worldly law is bidding us to compromise on His truth and Spirit. Compromise will weaken or even destroy the faith and commitment of His saints. Those who decide to protect their hearts and faith will find safe traveling in keeping His Word and acknowledging His Ways, even as the number of their traveling companions grows smaller and smaller.

Our family determined that the eternal paths mentioned in verse six of Jeremiah were not the ways we had been following in the Church as we knew it. He lured us into exploring God's original pathways for the church and for Israel. He began this journey by directing us to the book of Leviticus chapter 23. There in those verses He gave us a glimpse of Himself unadulterated by man's traditions and cultural doctrines. We were excited to see where the sincerity of His pure Word might lead us. He began to speak to us about becoming fishers of men and we pictured ourselves traveling in the fishing boat with Jesus in the wake of His Old Testament teachings for Israel. We knew that these teachings were shadows that had been magnificently designed to foreshadow the coming of Jesus. They were meant to train His people to recognize Him when He came as flesh and dwelt among them. We also knew that Israel had periodically and consistently wandered off the eternal path and into trouble. Their pattern reminded us of our own wanderings and we had hope that, similarly to the Israelites according to Jeremiah, our going back to the eternal, 'good old way' might straighten our walk out and realign us onto the narrow path that had at one time been called The Way.

My husband and I faced a problem, also described in 1 Corinthians 3:1-7, when we began to pull away from the denominational church we had belonged to for eight years. The resistance came first from our own hearts, then later from family and friends.

> *For while there is jealousy and strife among you, are you not of the flesh and behaving only in a human way? For when one says, "I follow Paul," and another, "I follow Apollos," are you not being merely human? What then is Apollos? What is Paul? Servants through whom you believed, as the Lord assigned to each. I planted, Apollos watered, but God gave the growth. So neither he who plants nor he who waters is anything, but only God who gives the growth.*
> (1 Corinthians 3:3-7)

Membership in a particular church can be wonderful and fulfilling; however, it can also become the source of our loyalty and that deep emotion can actually compete with the Holy Spirit as He leads us to move on. My husband's family had belonged to this particular type of church for many generations, and when we left there was a ripple effect that disturbed the team. Some even took our leaving to mean that we didn't want to do anything with them anymore or worse that we didn't care about them. We did not ever say these things and to my knowledge we didn't give this impression, but the act of leaving something so dear left questions that people answered for themselves incorrectly. I believe this is a reflection of what can happen in our hearts when God does something unexpected or seems to be absent in a situation or event and we feel wronged or deceived by Him. Our human instinct can kick in and cause our understanding to rise up and emotions to take over. We can become angry inside and feel like rebelling. What if we are supposed to look at these times differently than we have in the past? Perhaps these times of trial, change and suffering are actually essential times of growth for the church as individuals and as a body? Jesus learned obedience from the things He suffered (Hebrews 5:8) and so will we. On the flip side, if we avoid suffering, we won't learn obedience. Learning to submit our flesh to God's direction and authority appears to be intimately connected to our willingness to suffer in order to gain what He has for us:

> *While Jesus was here on earth, He offered prayers and pleadings, with a loud cry and tears, to the One who could rescue Him from death. And God heard His prayers because of His deep reverence for God. Even though Jesus was God's Son, He learned obedience from the things He suffered. In this way, God qualified Him as a perfect High Priest, and He became the source of eternal salvation for all those who obey Him.* (Hebrews 5:7-9)

Our human tendency to avoid suffering may be an element that has kept us from maturing in the Church. Our loyalties to job and church may be at times rooted in a desire to stay comfortable and in control, but what if our loyalty to denomination or leadership has actually caused the church to remain incomplete and unfulfilled? What if the fruit of the church is running dry because the people who were supposed to leave have stayed and the people who were supposed to come couldn't because the place they were to fill remained occupied?

Paul talks about this pattern of pruning and grafting-in when he describes how the original Church body was formed. In his letter to the Romans, Paul describes what happened to the Jews who would not believe. He parallels God's people, Israel with the branches that grow on a cultivated olive tree (Romans 11). Some of the branches of this cultivated tree were pruned because of unbelief. They lacked real faith in God. Gentile believers are described in this passage as branches from a wild olive tree that have been grafted to this cultivated tree. They have been grafted and established on this tree because of their faith in Jesus as the one true God. This incredible privilege granted to us through our faith in Jesus allows us the opportunity to share in the richness of the root and sap of the cultivated olive tree. Our position on this tree is completely dependent on our faith in Christ. Like Abraham, our faith must be in the true Seed who is Jesus Christ and will result in the fruit of Christ. That fruit is only possible from a heart humbled and fully turned toward their Savior and Lord, Jesus Christ. Paul warns us not to become boastful toward the branches that were pruned lest in pride we too become unfaithful. Humbleness is a key characteristic of God's faithful remnant.

> *Humbleness is a key characteristic of God's faithful remnant.*

In other parts of scripture believers are described as fruit on the true vine of Christ. In Him and He in us we are expected to produce the good sweet fruit of character that looks more and more like Jesus and less and less like our own human flesh. When persecution and trial come, in our natural self we will tend toward bitterness and self-focused righteousness. In John 15 Jesus is referring to his disciples and how they are to live their lives after He is gone-as branches on the vine. Up until then Israel had been referred to as the vine. Jesus makes it clear in one of His last lessons before His arrest and crucifixion that the true vine is Jesus. Everything having been made by Him and through Him and for Him (Romans 11:36) must continue to abide in Him in order to produce good fruit (John 15:4).God the Father, in this example, is the farmer of the vineyard where this precious vine grows. Israel as a people and a land are referred to as the cultivated plant that He formed and grew in His garden, expecting good fruit. When the owner of the vineyard (God) sent His servants (the prophets) to check on His garden and make sure it was maturing to produce good fruit, Israel persecuted and silenced them. Without this vital input from the prophets, which was to prompt hearts to repent and grow in love for God and each other, the garden grew bitter and useless. Finally, He (God) sent His own Son 'for surely they would invite Him,' His only Son, to partake of the fruit of His own vineyard. Yet, they would not and instead their self-interest and fear prompted them to kill the Son (Matthew 21:33-41).

When Peter, full of the Holy Spirit and power, testified to thousands on the day of Pentecost, God's power within him poured out the truth of the Gospel and 3,000 hearts were broken and turned toward God in repentance (Acts 2:37-42). Those 3,000 were now able to believe thus embracing God's Son as their Messiah. Other hearts, however, remained blind and were hardened toward the truth. Because of this unbelief, they were pruned from the vine and the Gentiles who did believe were grafted on the tree among the other believing branches (Romans 11).

Grafting a plant requires a cutting or wounding to take place as the old branches are pruned and the new are grafted in. In Romans 11, Paul warns those of us that were grafted in not to boast against the branches that were removed. In other words, do not think too much of yourself but instead, remember what He has forgiven us for and how easily we could doubt and sin again. Those wilting branches on the ground below His tree were cut off because of disbelief. Paul cautions us that the same thing could happen if we forget that we are supported by the root of the tree (Jesus). He encourages us to remain humble and thankful lest we too fall into the consequences of doubt and unbelief.

We can lose our place on the tree of Jesus' kingdom if we allow ourselves to doubt who He really is or misunderstand who we are when we are born again in Him. If we begin to suspect what the Word 'really' teaches us and replace it with what the world or false teachers say is true, we are in danger of being cutoff. In churches today, we can also lose our own opportunities for growth as well as jeopardize others if we are not growing in our understanding of His Spirit. The freedom and hunger for His way and for more of His Spirit can never be replaced by any other set of beliefs or interpretations. If we allow anyone or anything, whether church group or individual teachers, to replace His position in our hearts and lives we are at risk of disconnect from Him. Staying in a place out of loyalty to people rather than listening and obeying God risks our faith. We will only know what His will is for us if we are seeking His will with a freedom of spirit that has decided to submit humbly to Him, His Word and no one and nothing else.

> *What causes quarrels and what causes fights among you? Is it not this that your passions are at war within you? You desire and do not have, so you murder. You covet and cannot obtain, so you fight and quarrel. You do not have, because you do not ask. You ask and do not receive, because you ask wrongly, to spend it on your passions. You adulterous people! Do you not know that friendship with the world is enmity with God? Therefore whoever wishes to be a friend of the world makes himself an enemy of God. (James 4:1-4)*

It is only in being born again into Jesus that we become a part of God's new planting and in His planting we are all made new by the power of the Holy Spirit. Walking in the pure path of His Spirit there will be unity even though we come to Him with many different colors and cultures, traditions, and perspectives. This has been God's plan from the beginning and Paul warns us not to forget that He desires to regraft even the cut-off branches if they will repent and believe. This is the power of God's grace to those He has called. He gives us grace to do and believe what we would never be able to do or believe on our own.

I would never have believed that my husband and I would one day have a church in our home, but looking back I can see that God was ordering our steps in that direction from the beginning of our journey.

Each step we took in faith toward His will for our lives led us to the place we are in today. Each step we took in our own understanding and pride, delayed our progress. We have learned that staying humble and watching our step keeps the journey secure in Him. We have learned to watch for closed doors and not force our way through them. We have greeted open doors with caution until we determine that Jesus opened it and then we proceed through with joy. The doors that Jesus opens remain open and no one can shut them. The ones He shuts no one can open. Keeping our steps in faith and not our own sights keeps us from getting trapped in places we weren't ever supposed to enter.

Our family's church story begins with the pursuit of His purity, the baptism of the Holy Spirit, which occurred at different times and in unique manifestations for each of us. No one person has the exact formula for you. Jesus is the doorkeeper, and when we invite Him in to cross over our threshold and He eats with us, the meal will be uniquely gifted to us who He created. Just like the colors of His rainbow spectrum; red, orange, yellow, green, blue, indigo and violet, His gift of the Holy Spirit becomes real and full for each of us in different ways as He shares His gifts and talents as He sees fit and in His timing. Our responsibility in this relationship is to take whatever faith (trust) we have and use the gifts He has given us for His purpose, wherever and however that may be.

My grandpa's story of walking miles and miles to school through South Dakota blizzards and bull paths was more than just a tall tale to teach his grandchildren about character. It was a real example of how his heart was formed by those experiences. He valued the goal of those journeys which was to get to the one room school house where his mother was a teacher. He became the champion for the under-dog and perhaps that was because of what he saw his younger brother go through with the bull in the field they had to cross. God teaches us in similar ways. He lures us into the places where we don't have our usual resources at our disposal. Like parents who take their kids out camping so they can find out what is in them as they hand scrub the dishes and sleep on the ground, our Father in Heaven does the same thing. We can chose to hate and resent these experiences or love and trust them.

As we begin to obey and go into the wilderness to meet Him and be tested and tried, each of us will most likely find that He has provided a uniquely designed appointment. What will be the same about our time there is that each wilderness experience will be designed by God to grow His Spirit in us, taking from our souls what is not His and replacing it with His characteristics. Those are the pearls of our journeys into the lonely and desolate places of our lives and thoughts. If we avoid the wilderness we are actually avoiding our growth in Him. His goal is that we develop the mind of Christ more and more in our lives. If we aren't seeing this growth manifested in more love, joy, peace, patience, kindness, goodness, faithfulness, gentleness and self-control (Galatians 5:22-23), it may be that we missed Him somewhere along the way. If this is the case, we need to repent, seek Him, and find out why we have stopped growing.

Failure to recognize the true condition of our hearts through trials can create a 'dangerous slope' in which we can begin to resist His presence within us. This can develop into the lukewarm faith mentioned in Revelation:

> I know your [record of] works and what you are doing; you are neither cold nor hot. Would that you were cold or hot! So, because you are lukewarm and neither cold nor hot, I will spew you out of My mouth! For you say, I am rich; I have prospered and grown wealthy, and I am in need of nothing; and you do not realize and understand that you are wretched, pitiable, poor, blind, and naked. Therefore I counsel you to purchase from Me gold refined and tested by fire, that you may be [truly] wealthy, and white clothes to clothe you and to keep the shame of your nudity from being seen, and salve to put on your eyes, that you may see. Those whom I [dearly and tenderly] love, I tell their faults and convict and convince and reprove and chasten [I discipline and instruct

> *them]. So be enthusiastic and in earnest and burning with zeal and repent [changing your mind and attitude].* (Revelation 3:15-19)

This lukewarm faith can look like the carelessness of Esau who sold his blessing for the pleasures of his stomach. This is exactly what happened to the Pharisees and Sadducees of Jesus' day. They had grown content, complacent and prosperous in their positions by allowing their hearts to harden to the situation of God's sheep placed in their care. Many of them found themselves grafted off of their own olive tree because of this lack of faith in the true Messiah who came but so many of them failed to recognize. Paul warns us of falling into the same prideful pit if we begin to boast of our positions and think less of those whose disbelief led them to be pruned off. It is a snare of the devil that convinces us to grow complacent and submissive to what is not holy in this world.

> *That no one may become guilty of sexual vice, or become a profane (godless and sacrilegious) person as Esau did, who sold his own birthright for a single meal.* (Hebrews 12:16)

Time is running out and many of the patterns we have fallen into cannot be counted on to redirect us from the pits in our path. Therefore He (Jesus) says to you, "Awake, O sleeper, and arise from the dead, and I shall shine (make day dawn) upon you and give you Light" (Ephesians 5:14). God has a word for all of us, He says; I will make your rooms and hallways full of My Light if you will seek Me with your whole heart. My Light is designed to reveal your sins and secrets, but don't be afraid or anxious when you see them. I do not show them to you to condemn or shame you; I show them to you so you can repent of them. In repenting, I get to show you how much I love you by forgiving you, cleaning up what they have done to you and teaching you how to stop doing them again. These areas of sin I am showing you weigh you down and keep us from being closer. Please do not feel as though you need to hide from these things that I have shown you. When you avoid what My Light exposes, you risk our time together running out, so look carefully then how you walk! Live purposefully and worthily and accurately, not as the unwise and witless, but as wise people, making the very most of the time—buy up every opportunity, because the days are evil. You don't need to continue to hide in the dark and shadows trying to step around those sins and secrets. I am faithful, I love you and I will help you. The feet of your children and their children that follow you will trip over the things you leave on the floor, making them fall and skinning their knees. Welcome the light I'm offering you and see what I see so we can clean up your room (which is your heart) and make it a safe and welcoming place for others to come and visit.

Therefore do not be vague and thoughtless and foolish, but understanding and firmly grasping what the will of the Lord is. I want you to be free my dear child, to do all that I have done and more on this earth. Trust me to keep your heart clean and pure, and I will show you greater things than you have imagined. I have work for us together out in the world; we will do it together with the help of the Holy Spirit. You will do greater things than I did in my time here. So do not get drunk with wine, for that is debauchery; but be continually filled and stimulated with the Holy Spirit. Think about how it looks to be continually filled. Picture your heart like a clay pot under a running spigot of water. His river never stops flowing—we can be filled to over flowing. In this place of abundance, speak out to one another in psalms and hymns and spiritual songs, offering praise with voices and instruments, making melody with all your hearts and at all times to the Lord, and for everything giving thanks in the name of our Lord Jesus Christ to God the Father (Ephesians 5:14-20).

He who is able to hear, let him listen to and heed what the [Holy] Spirit says to the assemblies (churches). (Revelation 3:22)

Chapter 2

TRUTHFULLY HIS

Faithful are the wounds of a friend, but the kisses of an enemy are lavish and deceitful (Proverbs 27:6).

If you look for truth, you may find comfort in the end; if you look for comfort you will get neither comfort nor truth only soft soap and wishful thinking to begin, and in the end, despair.
-C.S. Lewis

The False Church

THERE IS A deep pit of self-righteousness that is pervasive in the world today that claims Jesus was just another prophet among many. This is an ancient deception. It sounds just like the whisper of Satan into Eve's ear, "Did God really say not to eat that fruit?" Yes, God did say that and the serpent lured Eve into the lie of doubt and man fell into sin. God also told us that He would provide an answer to our sinful hearts and His answer was His Son, Jesus. We believe that Jesus is the only way to be saved from the consequences of our sins. He is the truth and He is the life and we acknowledge that He defeated both sin and death on the cross. We know that He was resurrected from death in order that we might be resurrected to life. We know that God did not create us for His wrath. He did not select us so that He could condemn us, but that we might obtain His salvation through our Lord Jesus Christ (the Messiah). He died for us so that whether we are alive or dead when Jesus comes to judge us we might live together with Him and share His life (1Thesselonians 5:9-10). We are called to go and make disciples of all nations teaching them the gospel truth of Jesus Christ, our Savior, the Messiah.

Those lies fed to Adam and Eve were seeds of hate and jealous protection of self and personal desires. Those same seeds in the hearts of men and women have led to divisions in the Church and in some cases, loss of the truth and centrality of Jesus. These seeds encourage a spirit that looks to itself rather than to God. This spirit is a fear of what other men might have that we don't and sets out to use others in order to secure its own needs and goals. It needs and fears people which contradicts God's directive to fear only Him. This same spirit murdered Abel, despised Noah, challenged Moses, Joshua and Caleb and rebuked and wanted to stone a woman caught in adultery and eventually killed Jesus, Stephen and most of the apostles. In one-way or another, I suspect that we all struggle with this spirit. We must learn in this struggle to worship God more than people so that we can stop needing them so much and love them more.

I grew up in a household that spoke of the wonder of God, especially in nature. I learned the parable of the mustard seed at a young age and my mother would often point to the sky where the sun beams shone down through the clouds making a ladder that she assured me would lead people to Heaven. It was a childlike faith that she carried for God and it planted a small seed in my heart that would eventually prove the mustard seed parable true. These childhood stories would one day grow into a large tree of faith. First, however, there would be testing and proving. Through the years worldly influences led me to believe that Jesus could be represented by all different religions and similarly, that the God of all those religions was the same God as Christ. For example, Buddha was the Buddhist Jesus, Mohammed was the Islamic Jesus, Shiva was the Hindu Jesus, and so on. I was taught that they all just represented different characteristics of His holiness and that all paths led to the same God.

It was within this distorted and false understanding of God the Father and Jesus the Son that I began teaching world geography and government in the public schools of Pennsylvania. I was essentially a version of Paul when he was still acting as Saul. This doctrine I followed is called Universalism, and I held tightly to this team of universal believers, warring passionately against any who would contend with me about its truth. I harbored within my soul a need to be included and important in the human race, and for a long time this team of worldly thinkers met my need. It felt right in my heart to make sure everyone felt accepted and okay no matter what they were doing or believing to be truth. At the exact same time that I professed these lies, I also professed to be Christian and to believe in Jesus.

The deception was very real, though I did not recognize it at the time any more than Paul recognized before his Damascus road experience that he was being used to hurt the Church. To believe any of these false doctrines requires that we create our own definition of God or choose to believe someone else's creation of God. It cannot be the definition that the Bible shares which rightly portrays God as He is, which is holy and pure. His ways are right and good, while our own hearts are deceitful and selfish and out for our own perception of what is good.

That these same hearts live in defiance of Him until they are born again in Jesus His Son was never taught to me or else I managed to miss this essential message, even in the church. These self-created definitions of Christianity deny the truth of the Creator of our souls. They rebuff His plan for all to know of His good news, which teaches that we can all be included and thriving on His vine and that way is through faith in Jesus Christ His Son as our Savior and Lord. God's will is for all to be included, and He has provided the only way the human race will ever accomplish it—salvation through Jesus Christ, His Son (Ephesians 2).

Saul's world was severely shaken when he encountered Jesus on the road to Damascus. Mine too was challenged one day when a courageous and faithful student in my public school classroom included a tract about being born again in her Christmas card to me. She was an exemplary young lady, one who was humble and worked hard and always told the truth. Picture Mary, from "Little House on the Prairie"—if you have ever seen that television program or read the books—that kind of young lady. I respected her as a student and admired her as a person. She cared enough about me as her teacher to risk including that tract in my card.

I remember picking up an offensive feeling at first as I quickly shelved the tract in a box where I kept special cards from my students, family and friends. I wondered briefly why she thought I wasn't a Christian. The tract read "Would you like to become a Christian?" I rationalized that she didn't get it and I sympathized with her simple understanding of the world. That is called a spirit of pride (mine).

This lie of relative truth and compromise—in order to be 'inclusive' of more people—holds strong sway in many churches and reflects the world's move toward a false unity. We unwittingly welcome this lie into our homes where it thrives in well meaning, unredeemed hearts. The only true unity comes from a once-selfish heart that has been broken and cried out for help and found Jesus answering. If that same heart chooses to repent of its selfish, sinful nature and invite Jesus to teach it how to live it can truly be alive and unified in Christ. In this humbleness of heart, the Spirit of God will come to live and grow, teach and counsel until we begin to have a mind like His. We have unity in and through His Spirit which we receive when we ask Jesus to be Lord of our lives (born again in Him). We cannot create a false unity through programming or professional planning or human desire no matter how well intended. We can do nothing apart from Christ (John 15:5).

My great grandmother was a believer and follower of Jesus Christ and she raised three sons on the western frontier of the United States. As a teacher in a one-room school-house, she wrote letters to Readers Digest describing the miracles she witnessed on Sundance Mountain. My grandfather, her middle son, gravitated toward the Universalist Church, and I think I know why. When he and his brothers left home to make a living for themselves, they brought their mother's heart with them for God's people but ultimately didn't find that same heart of love in the Christian churches they encountered. They didn't see the Jesus they had come to know through her in that one-room school-house. As the country was hit harder and harder by the financial and economic stress of the depression, they turned farther and farther from His heart and found themselves, I believe, facing what seemed best to their understanding—Universalism, which is man's version of inclusion and today excludes the truth of Jesus entirely.

These young men were modern day apostles, pastors and teachers who would spend their lives building highways across the west, developing and writing curriculum as superintendents' of schools and leading editing departments for large publishing houses in the east. One of them would hold a professorship at a large prestigious university in the Midwest. My siblings and I followed suit in our careers, using our God-given talents well and fruitfully for the most part in order to build our own (and our family's) kingdoms and reputations.

What happened in the Universalist Church is the same dangerous deception happening in many churches today. The Universalist doctrine initially set out to be fishers of men. They did this by providing a safe and totally inoffensive atmosphere in their services, teachings and worship. They embraced all religious beliefs as part of His good creation. The intent was that once in a trusted relationship, the good news would be preached and Jesus would float to the top. This is not what happened and, in fact, Jesus was never invited into their worship. The cross, hidden from view, became ineffectual and meaningless. Picking up our cross and suffering in order to learn obedience and submission was replaced with social works and human love.

Jesus accomplished on the cross what the law in the Old Testament could never do for us. He fulfilled our desperate need to be forgiven and cleansed from our sins by becoming a perfect Lamb as a sacrifice for our sins (John 1:36). Jesus' resurrection to new life offers us the greatest gift we can ever have, the choice to live in freedom from our shame and guilt caused by our sin. In Him and His gift of the Holy Spirit we are given the means to be forgiven and the power to learn to walk away from sin and into true life. If this teaching is not the central teaching in the church, then He is not invited. Slowly but surely, Jesus disappeared from teachings in these churches.

God is good and He has provided the answer to our sin problems but we must first recognize that we have a sin problem. He came to heal the sick but if we have convinced each other that we are not sick, if all sin is now 'legal' then why would we need Jesus? God the Father sent His only Son Jesus to be the answer to a human struggle over what is good and what is evil. As the world turns His Word upside down and inside out in order to make good evil and evil good, we must hold fast to the truth. He is the truth and His Word is everlasting. We must learn to see sin through His lens and His understanding not our own. He knows what is best for us and what will bring us true peace and the love we were all created by Him to seek and desire. We are all sinning, whether the world calls it ok or not, we are ill and many of us know it. Repent, ask Him to forgive, He is faithful to forgive and cleanse us if we will humble ourselves and repent and turn and sin no more (James 4:1-10). This is only possible through an intimate and thriving relationship with His Spirit, who is His power within us.

When I reached the age of seventeen I had experienced eleven moves to either different houses or different states or different countries. That's a move approximately every two years and in that kind of atmosphere I learned how to get very comfortable with change, even major change. When I see change coming, I start to prepare and let people know. On the flip side, however, I am not as good at prolonged periods of the same activity or environment. I get uncomfortable when things seem stagnant or still. I find myself struggling in the waiting while surrounded by 'the same.' My husband on the other hand, is a man of tradition and consistency. He loves routine and schedules and changes in them make him uncomfortable. He is a tradition keeper while I am a tradition breaker, and neither of us is necessarily wrong. God brought us together because as we struggle for unity we become a better representation of God's heart for our family. God is faithful and who He was is the same today and will be the same tomorrow. His mercies are new every morning and that fact means that while there are times to be changing things and a time to be waiting and staying, His peace is available in each act of faith and all along the path in between. Like the Israelites with the cloud by day and the flame by night (Exodus 13:21), we must be on watch and ready. His presence makes the process work for His good.

Differences between me and my husband initially caused a lot of conflict in our marriage as we got to know each other and tried to understand how change and scheduling felt to the other person. The goal of a godly marriage is to come together in unity with Christ, not necessarily to please each other or to raise up one or the other's traditions, but to love and respect each other through a unified love for and respect of Jesus Christ. The Church, like marriage, is supposed to come together in unity with its individual members taking steps toward each other through Christ who is the Spirit of truth. In His Spirit we are one and there are to be no walls of judgment or condemnation. As people, we tend to think our way is the right way, and we get into trouble finding reasons to make our way THE way. If we truly embrace that Jesus is the only way, it helps put all the rest in perspective and frees us to do what we were created to do which is to glorify Him!

> *As each of you has received a gift (a particular spiritual talent, a gracious divine endowment), employ it for one another as [befits] good trustees of God's many-sided grace [faithful stewards of the extremely diverse powers and gifts granted to Christians by unmerited favor]. Whoever speaks, [let him do it as one who utters] oracles of God; whoever renders service, [let him do it] as with the strength which God furnishes abundantly, so that in all things God may be glorified through Jesus Christ (the Messiah). To Him be the glory and dominion forever and ever (through endless ages). Amen (so be it). Beloved, do not be amazed and bewildered at the fiery ordeal which is taking place to test your quality, as though something strange (unusual and alien to you and your position) were befalling you. But insofar as you are sharing Christ's sufferings, rejoice, so that when His glory [full of radiance and splendor] is revealed, you may also rejoice with triumph [exultantly].* (1 Peter 4: 10-13)

I remember vividly the day when I understood that I needed to be born again in order to truly begin my life with Jesus. What I realized was that church life as I was experiencing it was not working for me because I could tell I wasn't growing up into a nicer and kinder person who was closer to her husband. As a matter of fact, when things would go wrong in my life or my children's lives, I found myself reacting to the pressure with more anger and bitterness than ever before. This repeated behavior problem was separating me farther from my family. It felt to me that during times of trial I would tear down everything I had worked to build in my family and my marriage. I wore my sins right out in the open, on my sleeves for everyone to see, and words would fly right off my sharp tongue and light a fire to those very things I had carefully built and treasured just the hour before (Proverbs 14:1). I was hungry and desperate to find a cure; I wanted to become an excellent wife and godly mother.

My heart problem became obvious to me at an extended family get-together. Someone I considered a friend and mature Christian made an unexpected comment to me during that visit, which would be the instigation I needed to make a change.

I was standing in front of the refrigerator looking at a picture taken several years before of my daughter and myself. In the picture I was wearing a slightly snug red sweater and boasting a much bleached blonde head of hair. A toe ring was also visible, and glittering in the light of a campfire were multiple, purposefully showy, loop earrings. What I could not get my eyes off of was not those things but my little girl, smiling gleefully up at me as we roasted marshmallows for s'mores. That same little girl was now a pre-teen and earlier that morning had locked herself away from me in her room, suffering under the pressures of school demands, church expectations, and our own divided homes. She hadn't made it to this family get-together and I had been alright with that. Social functions, as it turned out, were the one thing in which I felt I could give her some freedom of choice.

As I looked at the picture, I realized that somewhere in the past few years I had stopped fighting for the truth of Jesus and His love. I had given in to the doctrines and demands of people. In particular, I had stopped pursuing His Sprit and His discipline and exchanged it for duties, and the ungodly disciplines of shame, scoffing, and manipulation. What had once been my battle cry on behalf of Him in my life and marriage, had somewhere along the way been lost to the fear of man. I had grown bitter over the loss of that battle, and I suddenly realized why I had a pit in my throat all the time. I was a fraud, and I desperately wanted to get back to the gift of love that I could see in me in that picture.

I was daydreaming my way into that picture wishing I could retrieve that day and restore the innocent love between a mother and her trusting, gleeful little girl when my friend, leaned over to me and said: "It's just amazing how much you have changed since that picture! I can't believe how you were then. You are so much better now!" She meant well by what she said. In some ways, my current outward appearance did seem to better represent a pious heart for God. But it wasn't true of what was inside me or anything else in my life at that point. I remember staring intently at the picture trying to see what could possibly have needed changing in that scene; it was so much better than being the fake I had become! I had fallen into a pit in the path I had taken, and Satan whispered into my ear at the refrigerator: "Ha ha! I won and Jesus lost! You allowed me to steal your love, kill your marriage, and destroy your family! And all I had to do was get you to think that people were right about you!"

At the time the picture on the refrigerator was taken (see above paragraph) I was well-established in the world, well liked, and successful. I had my own house and a great career. I had first met Jesus at a church camp in Pennsylvania when I was fourteen but then we moved to a different state. My mother had taught me enough about Him that when divorce launched its assault against me when my daughter was three, the struggle had broken me to the point of crying out to Jesus for His mercy. He had graciously walked me through the darkest hours of my life as I negotiated for the rights of my child and attempted to exit a marriage where I had grown to be afraid for all of our safety. Jesus had been faithful. I was growing madly in love with Him when I met my second husband; but I was not born again, therefore I was not sealed with the Holy Spirit, and Satan knew that made me a target.

My heart at that moment by the refrigerator felt the pounding of Satan's arrogant, judgmental hammer, and I felt myself becoming aware that I had once again, fallen into a pit of my own making. My heart, once gleeful and expectant of the good I might bring and enjoy in my new

Truthfully His

marriage and family had been poisoned by disappointments and failed attempts to make people pleased and happy. Unmet expectations and desires lured me into living in a darkening pit that eventually controlled me. Listening to Satan convinced me to stop trying or even enjoying what I did have in my life and left me looking only at the shriveled pits of half-eaten fruit. What we stare at long enough or that which we have fear of eventually forms into an idol in our souls, and we begin to act like whatever it is. I had developed a fear of man that took over my awe of God and I had allowed this fear to wound me. This wound became an infection that spread to my whole family as I became less and less loving and joyful. As I became convinced that people were right about me, bitterness and disappointment in myself hardened my heart into a stony, protected, and withdrawn shell. I would never be able to satisfy Satan's expectations of me, he was right about that, so I gave up. Satan will NEVER be satisfied with what we try to do to please him. I thought the people I was trying to please represented Jesus' expectations of me, but they did not. They only represented their own needs and desires for love. I had been fooled. I had forfeited the real love of Christ and was spreading defilement throughout my body and sharing it with others.

Defilement is like sewage that we step in and don't realize is on our shoe until we have spread it all over the house. I was experiencing extreme depression to the degree that I almost couldn't parent and I know I wasn't being a very good wife. Depression and anxiety had infected the children and was manifesting in poor choices in friends, low grades, angry outbursts and self-harm. I realized that we were in fact, near to spiritual death. My castle was about to fall, and I needed to relocate fast! I could leave as I had left my first marriage, I could convince my husband to move away from the people that so overwhelmed me, or I could let Jesus relocate me to His rock from where I would never have to move again.

I went home that night, pulled out the tract given to me by my student years before in the Christmas card, and with all my might I prayed that prayer.[1] Tears ran down my face as I asked Jesus for forgiveness and to be born again. I begged Him to make me new and to heal my marriage and our family because I now understood I was not the answer.

I had no idea that night what I was doing, but some of you reading this know that when you ask Jesus to begin a work in you and your home He is faithful to forgive and cleanse, and that is just what He did over the next ten years. Jesus had knocked, I had heard Him and invited Him in, and that evening He began to teach me what it means to give your heart to the Savior of the world.

> *Those whom I love, I reprove and discipline, so be zealous and repent. Behold, I stand at the door and knock. If anyone hears my voice and opens the door, I will come in to him and eat with him, and he with me. The one who conquers, I will grant him to sit with me on my throne, as I also conquered and sat down with my Father on his throne. He who has an ear, let him hear what the Spirit says to the churches.* (Revelation 3:19-22)

This incident at the refrigerator was one of the keys that turned our family around from filling our plates with religious works to filling our souls with His love. Our goals had been aimed at pleasing people in our lives. These goals were based on values that rewarded effort whether they were God directed efforts or not. Work itself is not bad as long as it is directed in faith generated by Jesus (Romans 14:23). By the time this incident occurred, the works I had filled my plate with were ones that pleased me or other people but didn't include God's input at all.

He had been nudging us that something was wrong and we had been stubbornly holding onto our familiar routines even though they had gotten us stuck in a pit. Jesus was ready to move away from this

---

[1] Dear Lord Jesus, I know that I am a sinner, and I ask for Your forgiveness. I believe You died for my sins and that you were resurrected from the dead. I turn from my sins and invite You to come into my heart and life. I want to trust and follow You as my Lord and Savior. In Your Name, Amen.
Prayer from *Steps to Peace with God*. www.BillyGraham.org 1-877-247-2426.

wrong path and show us a better way. We had been dangerously close to making a choice to stay in the dark, familiar pit instead of taking the risk to make changes that the light would certainly reveal were necessary.

> *This is the crisis we're in: God-light streamed into the world, but men and women everywhere ran for the darkness...because they were not really interested in pleasing God. Everyone who makes a practice of doing evil, addicted to denial and illusion, hates God-light and won't come near it, fearing a painful exposure. But anyone working and living in truth and reality welcomes God-light so the work can be seen for the God-work it is.* (John 3:19-21, The Message)

Once God moves on to the new, you will find holding onto the old to be fruitless and sometimes dangerous. In this new season, I geared-up to embrace change. I knew how to do that part! Being so busy with seemingly good works when you aren't spending at least that same amount of time—if not double the time—in prayer and in the Word is a recipe for disaster, and it had opened us up to deception. I set my attention on prayer and lots of journaling about prayer.

God really does know everything that is going on and all those days and weeks that I had been filling our plate with self-motivated work God had also been at His work. One of our children had been growing sadder and sadder, spending increased time lying on their bed all-alone in their room. God knew what they were thinking about and why they were thinking it. But when God woke me up in the middle of the night to tell me to dump all the alcohol in our house, it didn't make sense to me. This walk we had chosen took us on a path where we were to be led by the light of His love. The idea of unconditional love and unconditional submission (trust) to the source of that love was all very new for me. When the light of Jesus' love revealed that there was a truth called alcoholism blocking our ability to take the next step on His path of healing I rejected it as unsubstantiated (no facts to convince me) and

I promptly turned back to my own understanding. My own darkened knowledge reminded me that all that alcohol down in our cabinet had cost a lot of money. I feared that my husband would not approve of just dumping it, especially with no practical explanation.

I also rationalized that by the world's standards I didn't have a problem with alcohol and certainly my husband didn't. I thought this was about me, and it never dawned on me that this had to do with our children and the healing of our family that I had been praying to God about only days before. With no practical need that I could see for God to have requested this of me, I decided to ignore His still small voice that had awakened me to warn me and guide me. Wrapped in my comfortable darkness, I went back to sleep.

> *This is the crisis we're in: God-light streamed into the world, but men and women everywhere ran for the darkness...because they were not really interested in pleasing God.*

Hearing isn't just mentally registering that God has said something, it includes accountability for what we hear. He wants us to both understand and discern from what we are hearing. It requires lots of time with Him, uninterrupted time of listening and being quiet before Him. It takes making mistakes and finding out that He was right and it didn't matter what you understood—you should have just obeyed in faith. These are some of the true works of faith, when we step out into the sea and it doesn't make a lick of sense and to our surprise, He parts it.

All of our children had always been so careful and considerate of each other and us as parents, and we loved them all so desperately. They were always trying to make decisions that would please us, and they hated disappointing anyone. This can be a godly desire in the right environment, but when you live in a blended and dysfunctional family where Christ is not the center someone is going to get hurt and disappointed.

Children in these circumstances will keep trying to say all the right things, even when on the inside their hearts are drying up and hardening in the futility of the effort to keep all these people in their lives relatively happy. Our children knew why God would have me dump the alcohol, but when I shared the story no one wanted to tell me. That was okay because I didn't know it at the time, but God had just given all my children, and especially one, a chance to see how God knew them and loved them. This is such an amazing part of serving Jesus; even in our disobedience, He can turn it for the good.

Is Jesus Really Invited?

Jobs, sports, school schedules, events, cultural and religious expectations all put huge tolls on our relationship with our Savior, just like they put huge tolls on our relationships with our spouses and our children. Society and its worldly desires have profited exponentially at the expense of Jesus in our lives. Traditional Christian celebrations such as Christmas and Easter in many cases seem to have become largely worldly and universal. These times of the year, in particular, for us as blended families were like entering arm wrestling tournaments with each other. We would train for months anticipating the grueling conflicts of answering: "Whose turn is it to get so and so, when, and on what day?" No one was ever going to be completely happy no matter who was the most generous or most manipulative.

Even for intact families not torn by divorce, these seasons can become full of strife, worry and conflict. I question in some cases whether Jesus is really in these celebrations anymore. Are we as a society keeping these traditions for other reasons and simply pretending that He has been invited? This was a revelation to me that we who call ourselves Christians could pretend to invite Jesus to supper but never actually want Him to cross our thresholds. It would be the same as telling someone that we had invited "so and so" to our party, but we really hoped they would not come. The reality would be that we didn't actually want "so and so" there, but we wanted to appear to be the kind of people that included them. This is the presumption that 'pretend inviters' work under. We convince ourselves that we have actually invited Jesus into our lives because we attend church every week or are busy at church or we deem ourselves relatively 'good' people. We pretend that we love Him because we are doing everything our parents, family, world or church tell us to do. The facts appear to line up and we present them as evidence that we are Christians. The expectation, then, is that because we are making all these showings of love that He will show up when we need Him, but not hang around and bother us when we don't.

> *Once we agree we are Christians when we are not it follows that who Jesus is quickly becomes someone He is not.*

Once we agree we are Christians when we are not it follows that who Jesus is quickly becomes someone He is not.

I had asked Jesus to help my family heal; yet, I didn't obey Him when He told me what to do with the alcohol. Had I really invited Him in or just pretended to? I had a picture in my head of how a healed and united family would look, but was I willing to pay the cost it would take to get there? In my own limited ability to understand what healing would require and my utter disobedience to His command, He still continued to be at work in all of our hearts.

A human designed Jesus is who we are pretending to invite into our churches when we change the Bible to suit our personal picture of how His work should look, or how people should be acting, or what goes on in politics. He is the Word made flesh and He is a Holy God; we can't just change Him up to suit our needs, desires, or expectations.

Our much loved Pastor at the first church we attended, the pastor under whom we raised our older children, shared the following with me one evening during a church meeting. He held up the Bible in front of his face and said:

> "Courtney, there are two ways to look at the Word and interpret it. There are people who will live their lives as they like and prioritize family, job, personal pleasure, and even ministry before the Word. They will interpret the Word by the way they prefer to live their lives. On the other hand there are those who prioritize the truth of His Word and Spirit. They want to learn to love Him more than anything else. These people will interpret the Word through the Spirit and will attempt to live their life lined up with what they believe the Word teaches."

He added,

> "We want to be the second type of person."

I agree and I believe that this is what God asks of us when He asks us to be purely His; to love the Lord your God with all your heart, soul, mind and strength and then to love your neighbor as you love yourself (Matthew 22:37).

A few weeks later, Jesus woke me up once again with a firm conviction to dump all the alcohol in our house, and this time I obeyed. At three in the morning, I found myself downstairs taking a step into a sea I didn't even know needed to be parted—I dumped it all. Later that morning, the kids found out I had dumped the alcohol, and at least one of them knew why. God had put a righteous fear in one of my children that day because they knew what we did not, that drinking had become their drug of choice.

Chapter 3

PEACEFULLY HIS

He was wounded for our transgressions, He was bruised for our guilt and iniquities; the chastisement [needful to obtain] peace and well-being for us was upon Him, and with the stripes [that wounded] Him we are healed and made whole. (Isaiah 53:5)

BUNCHES OF GRAPES
By Walter Ramal

"Bunches of grapes," says Timothy;
"Pomegranates pink," says Elaine;
"A junket of cream and a cranberry tart
For me," says Jane.

"Love-in-a-mist," says Timothy;
"Primroses pale," says Elaine;
"A nosegay of pinks and mignonette
For me," says Jane.

"Chariots of gold," says Timothy;
"Silvery wings," says Elaine;
"A bumpity ride in a wagon of hay
For me," says Jane.[2]

---

[2] Ramal, Walter. "Bunches of Grapes." *Cambridge Book of Poetry for Children.* Edited by Kenneth Graham. G.P. Putman's Sons, 1916.

If we have accepted Christ as our Savior and asked Him to be Lord of our life by repenting of our sins and asking for His forgiveness, then we have taken up residence on His vine. Chances are we are not a lone branch of grapes. Rather we are one in a bunch of grape branches. Grapes grow close together and they affect each other in major and minor ways. Our family is known as a blended family, what a grape farmer might call his variegated variety. Our three oldest children, from the age of five, eight and nine all learned the dubious skill of navigating back and forth from one set of parents' houses to another. Week after week, our precious children, our grapes, if you will, were tended by one vinedresser and then another. Some vinedressers were faithful to Jesus' garden and others were faithful to different vineyards entirely.

> *I am the Vine; you are the branches. Whoever lives in Me and I in him bears much (abundant) fruit. However, apart from Me [cut off from vital union with Me] you can do nothing. If a person does not dwell in Me, he is thrown out like a [broken-off] branch, and withers; such branches are gathered up and thrown into the fire, and they are burned. (John 15:5-7)*

God's Garden

Jesus desires that we all be firmly planted in His vineyard, which is well provided for with the best soil conditions, sun exposure and protective walls and gates. He wants all of our attention, our heart, our energy, our strength, our minds, everything to be in Him alone. He promises that if we allow ourselves to totally trust Him, we will have abundant fruit. The fruit Jesus looks for and expects from His children is defined in the book of Galatians as the fruit of the Spirit, which is love, joy, peace, patience, kindness, goodness, faithfulness, gentleness and self-control.[3] This is the fruit our Savior looks for from His good vineyard, and He promises to

---
3 The Fruit of the Spirit's Not a Coconut. www.youtube.com/watch?v=8j2PUWQa7fs is a fun song we used to teach our children the fruits of the Spirit.

give us everything we need in order to produce a nutritious harvest. We submit to His will in this when we agree to practice abiding in Him.

> *So everyone who hears these words of Mine and acts upon them [obeying them] will be like a sensible (prudent, practical, wise) man who built his house upon the rock. And the rain fell and the floods came and the winds blew and beat against that house; yet it did not fall, because it had been founded on the rock. And everyone who hears these words of Mine and does not do them will be like a stupid (foolish) man who built his house upon the sand. And the rain fell and the floods came and the winds blew and beat against that house, and it fell—and great and complete was the fall of it.* (Matthew 7: 24-27)

Sounds simple until that north wind blows into the garden and the grape bunches are strained and stretched with each gust. These are the winds that God allows to blow in order to test our faith, and I know they will blow into your garden just as they have for our family. The deeper we learn to abide in Him, the more united we become. God desires closer and closer unity. The closer we get to each other, the more we interact, causing more friction. The more friction there is the hotter it gets. Rising hot air attracts cooler air and makes wind. This is true scientifically of the molecules that make up everything around us, and it is true spiritually of those of us that make up the body of Christ. Look at the disciples' lives with Christ. Three years of living, learning and working together created plenty of unity and friction. By the time they were praying together during Pentecost the heat they produced in the Spirit brought the powerful wind of the Holy Spirit. The examples of the early Church praying together in the book of Acts point to their unity in prayer and purpose and describe how it was accompanied by wind. Strong winds can bring storms, and storms are one way God tests our hearts for faith. In the Book of James we are told to count it all joy when we are enveloped in various trials and troubles because this is how our faith is tested and proven. Notice it does not say *if* we are enveloped in trial, but instead clearly warns us that trials are part of our walk by saying *when* we are in trial. If we patiently endure when these trials and troubles come, he assures us we will be fully developed in Christ with no defects (James 1:4-5).

I grew up dreading the winds that would inevitably blow through our house. It wasn't that I would not go through anything tough; our family had its share of hard times, but it was a mindset that I had developed that said no person should suffer if they didn't have to. Where I could avoid suffering, I would choose to avoid it. Where I could help others avoid suffering, I would do everything in my power to help them avoid it too. I would eventually discover much later in life that avoiding trials was not God's plan for His children. His pursuit of our hearts and His desire for them to produce good fruit for His kingdom requires that we learn obedience through suffering. The storms that God allows us to go through are designed to reveal our true heart condition. In our fallen state the sinfulness in our hearts require His light to reveal the true nature of our heart and soul. Where Satan is permitted to blow His wind, we are asked to turn toward Jesus and learn to abide only in Him. Believing by faith even in the midst of calamity that He remains in control.

> *I form the light and create darkness, I make peace [national well-being] and I create [physical] evil (calamity); I am the Lord, Who does all these things.* (Isaiah 45:7)

In learning to submit in Christ to these trials and afflicting storms, I've discovered perhaps a small part of what James means when he tells us that we can count our trials as joy. He often shows me His heart and ways in the work I do in my own backyard.

Our family decided to plant corn one year in our garden. We were instructed to make sure that the rows were at least five plants on a side, with each about a foot apart. We were told to plant the seeds in good soil and to make sure the corn was in the ground well before the middle of June. In most states that would not be a question, but in Minnesota where we live, the middle of June can still be pretty cold. We followed all the instructions and had our seeds in the ground by early June and small plants had already grown up by the end of that month. One day, as I glanced out our back door, I realized that a strong wind had picked up and was really pushing at our little corn shoots.

A typical June in Minnesota is truly the last month of spring, and as the sun starts to heat up things, the winds can be pretty strong. As I watched, I realized that some of the little plants were practically being uprooted. I went outside and began working the soil around each of them until I had managed to stabilize each plant and secure around its bottom a dirt mound that would help it stand stronger through the next windy day. This went on for about a week until the winds died down. July and August brought true summer. In October the corn stalks were now taller than I was and had promising ears on each of them. We were looking forward to corn on the cob when the fall winds began to blow. These late-year winds are harsher winds, blowing in the cold air that would soon carry snow and ice, for which our state of Minnesota is famous.

The corn—having made it through the spring winds and mounded well by the dirt I had packed around the stalks—developed good, strong roots during the summer. This corn would not be easily uprooted. We had weeded, watered, fertilized, and battled the bugs and were confident we had a good chance of producing quality corn. One day, just before the fruit was ripe, a strong windstorm blew in from the north. The corn stood strong; its deeper roots holding tightly to the soil allowed the stalks to sway gently in place. Three or four weaker stalks toppled to their sides but didn't fall completely to the ground. They had been caught by the stronger stalks beside them as though they had been dipped over by their partners in some kind of dance step. The silky tops of the cobs balanced safely off the ground and their roots, though stretched, were still planted securely in the soil.

This is how God works with those of us that are grafted into His vine. He tills, plants, fertilizes, and weeds us until we become the promise of a precious harvest of His good fruit. Without those warm winds in June, the corn stalk roots would not have been forced to dig in and become secured; they would have been weak and vulnerable when the stronger winds came in the fall. In our own lives, the more our 'roots' are accustomed to digging into His rich soil, the more peace we will have when the strong winds of trial and suffering blow our way. This peace will accompany us no matter where He sends us. If we are obeying God in faith, His peace goes too.

My father was a chief executive of an international company, and he enjoyed what he did. His work ethic was enviable by the world's standards and he received promotions often. These upward moves within the company would inevitably involve relocating to another state or even sometimes another country. I soon became adept at packing up my life and moving at a moment's notice. The heartache of leaving behind friends and all that was familiar was usually soothed by the excitement and anticipation of discovering new places and new friends. This pattern continued until I reached high school, and the ache of leaving seemed deeper while the desire to start all over became more daunting. Hopeful anticipation was replaced by something dark inside me, something I wouldn't be able to define until much later in life. I found that my heart had encased itself in something like a shell. It was shaped like a heart but was unable to be touched or give touch to anyone else. My heart had learned about self-preservation and that people could choose hate instead of love, rejection instead of friendship. I began to hide my heart in this shell by attempting to be perfectly pleasing and/or invisible to anyone who happened to be around me. I found that in this hiding I was able to love less and, therefore, not ache so deeply. What had actually happened, however, was I had begun to ignore and reject myself. My heart thought it was safe because it didn't hurt or fear anymore, but what was really happening was I had cut myself off from any possibility of suffering that life and love inevitably bring. My heart in this state would eventually die. A dead heart cannot love, and what do we do if we don't love? We hate. We start by hating ourselves, and then that is all we have to give others.

Hate cannot abide on the vine of Jesus Christ and will not bring peace to His vineyard. While it might pretend to live there, it really can't because the love of Christ will find it out and expose it for what it truly is—a hardened heart. True love from Jesus Christ will always reveal hate and its fruits of bitterness and self-pity. Jesus will always deal with our hate by leading us into His paths of forgiveness and reconciliation. He is all about resurrecting us from death to a better life that loves with the eternal love of Christ. He can only do this if we invite Him in to do the work. Often we will not answer His knock on the door of our hearts because we have become so secure in our bitterness and hate that we believe we are safe there. Exposure seems too hard to face, and forgiveness impossible or even undesirable. Like the corn whose weaknesses were exposed in the Spring winds and required the farmer to strengthen them for the harsher Fall, we too must invite Him into our hearts if we want His winds to expose our darkened hearts and prepare us for the stronger storms that are coming. Only He can work us into His good planting and make our lives a fragrant garden for His Kingdom.

> *Therefore be imitators of God [copy Him and follow His example], as well-beloved children [imitate their father]. And walk in love, [esteeming and delighting in one another] as Christ loved us and gave Himself up for us, a slain offering and sacrifice to God [for you, so that it became] a sweet fragrance.* (Ephesians 5:1)

In the Book of Genesis, the spirit of Cain is the manifestation of the hate that can take hold of our hearts. Cain was jealous of the attention God gave Abel's offering. Cain could not be turned from his selfish anger and allowed his jealous heart to begin to hate. What we hate soon becomes something that controls our life and our choices. Cain chose to get rid of the object of his jealousy and killed his brother. How often do we in the Church do the same thing; faced with difficulty, our hearts rise up and we assume we know something and judge our brother to death.

When faced with a trial, our fears, jealousies, and rancor can make us frustrated because we are so busy spitting out the seeds and the pits of God's fruit that we forget to be thankful. It is such a privilege to have the opportunity to enjoy the product of His work (His fruit) in our hearts and the hearts of others. Trials can feel like we are grapes being stomped on or trees being pruned, but His goal is more prolific fruit, with better juice or finer oil. Fear of suffering, jealousy toward each other, and hate in our own hearts are some of the ways the enemy of our soul, Satan, attempts to use the same trials meant to strengthen and heal to instead steal, kill and destroy God's garden. Which way a trial goes, into more abundant life or death is largely up to us to choose.

Ephesians 5:1 says we are to be imitators of God as beloved children. Think about what that means and what we might be prone to imitate. We tend to act like what we are most familiar with, especially in the face of a trial. Do we imitate our Savior or our idols? Do we choose what He would choose or what we think we have the right to choose?

> *Blessed (happy, to be envied, and spiritually prosperous—with life-joy and satisfaction in God's favor and salvation, regardless of their outward conditions) are the merciful, for they shall obtain mercy! You, therefore, must be perfect [growing into complete maturity of godliness in mind and character, having reached the proper height of virtue and integrity], as your heavenly Father is perfect.* (Matthew 5:7, 48)

Our God is characterized by mercy; He is forgiving, tender, and compassionate. His goal for our hearts is that they would love like His, reaching completeness in Him through various trials and disciplines.

He does not want us to lack for anything we need in our life. He does not want our foot to stumble or our faith to waiver. When we become hard, harsh, and severe with one another, we have become just the opposite of the character of God.

> *So be merciful (sympathetic, tender, responsive, and compassionate) even as your Father is [all these]. Judge not [neither pronouncing judgment nor subjecting to censure], and you will not be judged; do not condemn and pronounce guilty, and you will not be condemned and pronounced guilty; acquit and forgive and release (give up resentment, let it drop), and you will be acquitted and forgiven and released. Give, and [gifts] will be given to you; good measure, pressed down, shaken together, and running over, will they pour into [the pouch formed by] the bosom [of your robe and used as a bag]. For with the measure you deal out [with the measure you use when you confer benefits on others], it will be measured back to you.* (Luke 6:36-38)

The disciples faced this kind of choice when they found themselves in the middle of the Sea of Galilee, and a strong storm rose up threatening to capsize the boat and drown them all. They responded to the storm as fishermen who had lived all their lives on the sea, and the familiarity and experience of its danger led them to fear. They had all just witnessed the miracle of Jesus feeding the five thousand people with just two loaves and three fish, but their lifelong experiences on the Sea of Galilee convinced them they were in trouble. The things we are used to through our own experiences in this world can have such a strong pull on our hearts that we end up resorting to old and familiar habits. Our 'self' and what it understands about the world can pull on our hearts so persistently that it can steal our peace if we let it. I believe the disciples were focused on their own understanding of the sea and it overwhelmed the faith they were just beginning to build in Christ. Their Savior was sound asleep in the stern of the boat seemingly oblivious to the storm and what the disciples feared was their imminent demise. Which did they choose, to trust and imitate Jesus or doubt and waiver in fear?

> *And the disciples came and woke Him, saying, Master, Master, we are perishing! And He, being thoroughly awakened, censured and blamed and rebuked the wind and the raging waves; and they ceased, and there came a calm. And He said to them, [Why are you so fearful?] Where is your faith (your trust, your confidence in Me—in My veracity and My integrity)? And they were seized with alarm and profound and reverent dread, and they marveled, saying to one another, Who then is this, that He commands even wind and sea, and they obey Him.* (Luke 8:24-25)

They panicked and accused Jesus of leading them all to their deaths. The disciples fought the stormy trial in their own understanding and followed the lead of those around them. They were frantic with fear while Christ was asleep and at peace. In Christ, we have a gift called 'grace', and this gift gives us the power from God to keep our peace where it would be otherwise impossible. He will handle the storms of our lives because we trust Him. The storms will increase as our faith increases. His grace activated by our faith in His power makes fear, and hate powerless because it reminds us that Jesus will handle all these evil tendencies. Therefore, with His Holy Spirit in us we have access to the ability to persevere peacefully through all trials and storms.

> *Little children, you are of God [you belong to Him] and have [already] defeated and overcome them [the agents of the antichrist], because He Who lives in you is greater (mightier) than he who is in the world.* (1John 4:4)

Jesus came that He could carry the burden of our sinful hearts Himself and He died for us even while we were still sinners. He did not judge us as we deserved, and we are to imitate Him—doing what He says to do and saying what He says to say. He never wanted us to be focused on the trials, which can convince our flesh to rise up over our faith with fear and dread. Instead, He asks that we be totally focused on Him in every circumstance. He has not given us a spirit of fear, but instead, He offers us a Spirit of love, power, and a sound mind (2Timothy1:7). Abiding in this Spirit, which is His Spirit, guarantees our peace.

What are we afraid of? What freezes our heart and causes it to withdraw and hide from God's free gift of grace? If we can name our fears honestly, we will begin to win victory over them because abiding in His vine entitles us to ask for the help we need but don't deserve. He gives it, no questions asked. If we don't abide on His vine, we don't have access to this help. If we do abide on the vine but we don't ask, we won't have this help either. So this is where trials come in. They take us to a place which tests whether we are really abiding in Him or not. What He hopes we see is our own inability to persevere through the winds without Him; just like the corn could not make it without the farmer tending to its needs, neither are we to tend to our own needs and desires. He wants to be our all in all. What Jesus intends to grow through these trials is more faith and humbleness in our hearts. A heart cannot grow humbleness and faith while remaining hard. The more faith and humbleness we have, the more likely we are to turn only to Him for His help and to ask rightly. The humbled heart has compassion and seeks His help for the sake of love rather than selfish gain (James 4:1-4).

The key to our peace, then, is having our roots dug deeply into Him. This burrowing process happens when we are put through the winds of trial. If I attempt to avoid the suffering that trials bring, though I may be on His vine, I will never come to fully understand the peace of God that fills a heart deeply imbedded in Him. I will only know that the trial hurts and that I don't like to hurt, those are the facts. The truth is, He already died for any suffering I am going to go through, and the chastisement of my sin is upon Him (Isaiah 53:5). What He is saying in this verse, and many others, is that if I am truly abiding in Him, the suffering won't steal my peace. If I move mountains for the people around me, doing everything possible to alleviate their suffering and struggle, but don't help them to dig deeper into this peace, I am wasting my time and leading them astray (1Corinthians 13:2). Without a true abiding faith in Him and Him alone, the fact of their suffering will overwhelm their senses and hide His truth. His truth is found in the rich sap of His love. If I don't show others His love and only fix their problems they will not have what they need. Maybe not today, but eventually the winds and the rains will come. The floods will rise, and the truth of our foundation will be revealed. If the foundation is based on human love then our faith will collapse. If the foundation is built on His supernatural love, our faith will persevere and we will have life and have it abundantly.

> *The floods will rise, and the truth of our foundation will be revealed.*

The word *peace* in Hebrew is *shalom* and it means *health, security, tranquility, comfort, and clarity. The opposite of shalom is confusion, and war.*[4] Shalom can mean the absence of strife, but not always. It is more about the agreement and unity of our heart, soul, strength and mind with God's heart. The Bible tells us that Jesus is the King of peace, yet Jesus Himself assures us that He did not come to bring us peace as the world calls peace, but instead He brings a sword.

> *Therefore, everyone who acknowledges Me before men and confesses Me [out of a state of oneness with Me], I will also acknowledge him before My Father Who is in heaven and confess [that I am abiding in] him. But whoever denies and disowns Me before men, I also will deny and disown him before My Father Who is in heaven. Do not think that I have come to bring peace upon the earth; I have not come to bring peace, but a sword.* (Matthew 10:32-34)

---

[4] The Complete Word Study: Old Testament, King James Version. Zodhiates, Spiros, Th.D. AMG Publishers Chattanooga, TN 37422, USA. 1994. P. 2374. #7965 *Shalom.*

Christ does bring peace, but not as the world defines it or offers it. His peace is not a spirit of compromise with worldly ideas and understanding of love. Faith in the world's love will ultimately prove powerless and guarantees a lukewarm faith in Christ. Instead, God offers us an assurance of peace through His love for us that He showed us through His Son, Jesus Christ. It is our confident faith in Jesus' love for us that ensures our peace. His conquest over wrong, over Satan, and the triumph offered us at the cross is ours through our love of Him. This kind of love demands our loyalty to Him and will bring division even within families, communities, churches, and states (Matthew 19:29) because they compete for our attention and worship. Peace is not something we aspire to or strive for. That is the world's peace that will require us to be loyal to people rather than to God and will ask us to seek it at all costs including the forfeiting of the truth of the Gospel. God's peace, or shalom, is instead the blessing we receive in humble hearts completely sold out to the cross of Christ. The cross is God's answer to the devil's temptations of compromise. We who love Him pick up our cross and carry it, and in Him that burden is light. He will handle it because we trust Him.

Which will we choose? Is there something or someone that we allow to influence our choice for Christ? What gets between us and our ability to abide in Him, with Him, and for Him? What disrupts our sweet fellowship with our beloved Savior? If we desire His love for our own hearts and others, we need to answer these questions for ourselves. Have we heard His knock on the door of our hearts and have we answered it? If not, then something is keeping us from either hearing or opening that door. What is it? Perhaps we answered the knock and invited Him in only to show Him back out again. Why?

I was one who invited Jesus in, embraced His leading for a while during a particularly hard crisis in our family, and then promptly went back to status quo when the crisis settled down. I was no different than the disciples in that boat; I had seen manifestations of His ability to provide and protect.

Yet, as soon as I found myself back in a familiar setting and life became more like normal, I didn't know how to maintain the intimacy that I had known during the trial. I found myself slowly returning to my old ways; instead of pressing in and desiring more of Him, I settled for lukewarm faith.

Praise God, He just kept knocking, and His pursuit of my heart finally led me to take Him as my Savior. Once that very important decision is made, we become sealed with His Holy Spirit. Then, like the disciples in Acts, we are to seek to be baptized in His Holy Spirit. Finally, in the power of His baptism, we begin the walk of sanctification where the Holy Spirit begins to teach us to abide in Him all the time. These are the foundational pillars of our faith and are foreshadowed by three Jewish pilgrimage feasts:

1. Take Him as our Savior and be sealed with the Holy Spirit: Passover/Pesach

2. Seek baptism in the Holy Spirit (the full power of the Spirit): Pentecost/Shavuot

3. Abide in His presence all the time: Sukkot/ Feast of Booths

For to us a Child is born, to us a Son is given; and the government shall be upon His shoulder, and His name shall be called Wonderful Counselor, Mighty God, Everlasting Father [of Eternity], Prince of Peace. Of the increase of His government and of peace there shall be no end, upon the throne of David and over his kingdom, to establish it and to uphold it with justice and with righteousness from the [latter] time forth, even forevermore. The zeal of the Lord of hosts will perform this. (Isaiah 9:6-7)

The key to the heart of God is Jesus. He is love and the Holy Spirit is the guarantee of our salvation (Ephesians 1:14). In the Old Testament, the tabernacle in the wilderness was a structure built by the Israelites according to God's design given to Moses. It housed the Ark of the

Testimony, a beautiful, manmade but God-designed symbol of His holy presence among His people. The Ark held the Ten Commandments and was called by God, His mercy seat. It also held a golden jar with an omer[5] of manna and Aaron's rod that had blossomed.

There were two rooms in the tabernacle: the first room was called the Holy Place. In this room were found the table with the bread of His presence to feed the priests, the menorah with seven lamps representing the Holy Spirit, who is the Spirit of Christ, and the altar of incense where prayers were offered daily. The second room was called the Holy of Holies: this was where the Ark of the Testimony was kept and God's mercy seat where Moses and He would speak to each other. The two rooms were separated by a veil and Aaron, Moses' brother could not enter the Holy of Holies anytime he wanted, nor could anyone without God's permission or they would die. Aaron as High Priest had very clear directions to follow once a year to make atonement in the Holy of Holies for himself and the people (Exodus 25-40).

The veil separating the two rooms was a symbol of Jesus, when He died on the cross, the veil between the two rooms was ripped open from top to bottom, thus unlocking forever the door to the mercy seat (Matthew 27:51). We now can have access, through faith in Christ, to God's presence all the time. Jesus was judged righteous by His sinless life and in His death and resurrection, those of us who believe on Him for our salvation are judged righteous as well. We prove the truth of this righteousness by walking out our faith in Him each day.

---

5 The word *omer* is sometimes translated as *sheaf* –specifically, an amount of grain large enough to require bundling. The biblical episode of the manna describes God as instructing the Israelites to collect an *omer for each person in your tent,* implying that each person could eat an omer of manna a day. In the Instructions of Moses (the Torah in Hebrew), the main significance of the omer is the traditional offering of an omer of barley on the day after the Sabbath during the feast of unleavened bread (during the period of Temple sacrifice) as well as the tradition of the Counting of the Omer (sefirat ha'omer)- the 49 days between this sacrifice and the two loaves of wheat offered on the holiday of Shavuot. One Omer = 1/10 Ephah or an ancient Hebrew unit of dry measure equal to a little over a bushel or 3.64 litres.

> *But [that appointed time came] when Christ (the Messiah) appeared as a High Priest of the better things that have come and are to come. [Then] through the greater and more perfect tabernacle not made with [human] hands ... He went once for all into the [Holy of] Holies [of heaven], not by virtue of the blood of goats and calves [by which to make reconciliation between God and man], but His own blood, having found and secured a complete redemption (an everlasting release for us). For if [the mere] sprinkling of unholy and defiled persons with blood of goats and bulls and with the ashes of a burnt heifer is sufficient for the purification of the body, How much more surely shall the blood of Christ, Who by virtue of [His] eternal Spirit [His own preexistent divine personality] has offered Himself as an unblemished sacrifice to God, purify our consciences from dead works and lifeless observances to serve the [ever] living God? [Christ, the Messiah] is therefore the Negotiator and Mediator of an [entirely] new agreement (testament, covenant), so that those who are called and offered it may receive the fulfillment of the promised everlasting inheritance.* (Hebrews 9:11-15)

The book of Revelation speaks about seven churches that were literal congregations in the time of the Apostle John and could also represent different conditions we might find ourselves in individually and as the Church of Christ. The last of the seven churches mentioned in Revelation 3 is the church of *Laodicea*, which is a Greek word meaning a *people judged*.[6]

> *And to the angel (messenger) of the assembly (church) in Laodicea write: These are the words of the Amen, the trusty and faithful and true Witness, the Origin and Beginning and Author of God's creation: I know your [record of] works and what you are doing; you are neither cold nor hot. Would that you were cold or hot! So, because you are lukewarm and neither cold nor hot, I will spew you out of*

---

6 The Complete Word Study: New Testament, King James Version. Zodhiates, Spiros, Th.D. AMG Publishers Chattanooga, TN 37422, USA. 1991. P. 44&23. The Greek Dictionary of the New Testament. #2993, 2992, 1349. *Laodikeia, laos, dike.*

> *My mouth! For you say, I am rich; I have prospered and grown wealthy, and I am in need of nothing; and you do not realize and understand that you are wretched, pitiable, poor, blind, and naked. Therefore I counsel you to purchase from Me gold refined and tested by fire, that you may be [truly] wealthy, and white clothes to clothe you and to keep the shame of your nudity from being seen, and salve to put on your eyes, that you may see. Those whom I [dearly and tenderly] love, I tell their faults and convict and convince and reprove and chasten [I discipline and instruct them]. So be enthusiastic and in earnest and burning with zeal and repent [changing your mind and attitude].* (Revelation 3:14-19)

Jesus came the first time for the forgiveness of sins; He is coming again.. He does not want to find His church with hearts that have become lukewarm. He wants us doing what He has called us to do with all of our hearts, soul and mind. He wants us to have struggled in our callings to the point that we are only satisfied with Him and His presence in our lives. If we have compromised our hearts with the ways of the world or become satisfied with earthly rewards we have become lukewarm to our Lord. If we have allowed our hearts to be lukewarm, He warns us that we must repent and remember who He is and how He loves us or He will spit us out of His mouth (Revelation 3:16).

Many are called, few are chosen (Matthew 22:14). I believe that to be chosen requires that we walk through winds of trial and testing which challenge us to turn our hearts to Him in prayer and intercession. As we allow His winds to blow, they will fan the fire of His Spirit inside us and that will produce the heat of a fire hot enough to purify our hearts. A heart purified by God's fire has learned to clothe itself in His salvation and refuses to believe that they can clothe themselves in their own human efforts and good intentions. His heart will fill ours with a supernatural power called grace that fills us with His mercy, peace and love. This kind of heart desires only their bridegroom's face and is not intent upon His reward.

> *I will greatly rejoice in the Lord, my soul will exult in my God; for He has clothed me with the garments of salvation, He has covered me with the robe of righteousness, as a bridegroom decks himself with a garland, and as a bride adorns herself with her jewels.* (Isaiah 61:10)

An angel of the Lord reveals several important truths to John the Apostle about these seven churches. Each church is addressed individually with a message of how God sees them, warnings and discipline for each and His promises for them if they will believe and obey. The church of Philadelphia seems to have had their hearts changed in a way that greatly pleased God. The message for them was this:

> *And to the angel (messenger) of the assembly (church) in Philadelphia write: These are the words of the Holy One, the True One, He Who has the key of David, Who opens and no one shall shut, Who shuts and no one shall open: I know your [record of] works and what you are doing. See! I have set before you a door wide open which no one is able to shut; I know that you have but little power, and yet you have kept My Word and guarded My message and have not renounced or denied My name.* (Revelation 3:7-8)

The key of David is Jesus; by His death and resurrection, He has opened to those of us who will believe in Him the entrance to the true Holy of Holies. In this place, where our hearts come into contact with the fire of His presence, we are purified and changed for His glory. To become imitators of Christ and walk in love, we must learn to live life in His holy presence. There in His presence, He will talk to us about our hearts, judge us in His mercy, and give us the desire and ability to repent. He is faithful to forgive us and cleanse us. This is the true freedom offered by Christ, the freedom to purify our hearts through His love. This fills our hearts with His pure love, agape love, which is poured out for others as we minister, through the gifts given to us for

His Church. As He has loved us, we will come to love others, no matter our circumstance.

> *For the time [has arrived] for judgment to begin with the household of God; and if it begins with us, what will [be] the end of those who do not respect or believe or obey the good news (the Gospel) of God?* (1 Peter 4:17)

The door to the Holy of Holies accessed through Jesus will not remain open forever. Jesus' time as High Priest will end as He prepares to come again to judge the Church. When that time comes, He will change into His royal robes, and then we will all see Him as the King of Kings and Lord of Lords. So while we can, while He is near, let us go to the house of the Lord and spend time with Him, getting to know Him, and letting His heart change everything.

> We bow before You, our Lord and Savior, with our hands open and willing to release to You all and anything that You ask of us. No matter how great or how small, all we have is Yours.

He promises that in return He will bloom in our hearts a huge and glorious garden that will fill up every space we can see and even the places we cannot see. He will make of our hearts a garden to His glory.

> *For as [surely as] the earth brings forth its shoots, and as a garden causes what is sown in it to spring forth, so [surely] the Lord God will cause rightness and justice and praise to spring forth before all the nations [through the self-fulfilling power of His word].* (Isaiah 61:11)

Chapter 4

JOYFULLY HIS

You have made known to me the ways of life; You will enrapture me [diffusing my soul with joy] with and in Your presence. (Acts 2:28)

GLORIFY!

God tells us to glorify him. "Glorify" means "to make a big deal of." When someone makes a big deal of you, it fills up your heart with joy.

But why does God need us to make a big deal of him? Why does he need us to get joy?

He doesn't. In the beginning God the Father and Jesus, his Son, together with the Holy Spirit, were already there—a loving family, glorifying each other in this wonderful Dance of Joy.

No. God didn't create us so he could get joy—he already had it.

He created us so he could share it.

> He knows it's the thing your heart most
> needs to be happy. When God says,
> "Glorify me!" He's really saying, "Be filled
> With Joy!"
>
> He's inviting us into his Forever Happiness.
>
> "His secret purpose framed from the very beginning
> [is] to bring us to our full glory" **1 Corinthians 2:7 (NEB)**
>
> Taken from *Thoughts to Make Your Heart Sing* by Sally
> Lloyd-Jones&Jago, 2012 by Sally Lloyd-Jones. Use by
> permission of Zondervan. www.zondervan.com

I WONDER IF OUR society has a "give Google the glory" disease. Our pediatrician was the first one to introduce me to this epidemic when she told me that her patients were starting to come in to her office with pre-diagnosis from Google searches. She said that she spent more time talking them out of their worried expectations than she did examining them. When she discovered there wasn't anything to be concerned about she worried that they did not trust her as much as they did Google. I think we have a tendency to be exactly the same way with God.

I heard a story once about a frazzled mom who had a lot of children, and one day in the kitchen she sat down on the floor and started to cry. I don't think this is an unusual place for mothers to find themselves, but what this one did next is worth noting. She pulled her apron over her head and began to pray. Right there in the middle of her kitchen, she entered into her own personal tabernacle and closed the door.

> *But when you pray, go into your [most] private room, and, closing the door, pray to your Father, Who is in secret; and your Father, Who sees in secret, will reward you in the open. And when you pray,*

> *do not heap up phrases (multiply words, repeating the same ones over and over) as the Gentiles do, for they think they will be heard for their much speaking. Do not be like them, for your Father knows what you need before you ask Him.* (Matthew 6:6-8)

A lot of us would do well to take up this practice in our kitchens. As a mom, daughter, sister, cousin, granddaughter, aunt, and friend, and especially as a wife, I have found great joy in one very simple prayer "Jesus, help!" As soon as I call, He is by my side and the anxieties flee. God loves when His people cry out to Him from a sincere heart humbly emptied of all but Him. In this position we will find that we have all we need and more. His earnest desire is to give and serve unconditionally, pouring out to us more and more from His deep pockets of compassion and mercy. All He asks in return for sharing His abundance is our love, which results in our obedience expressed in joyful thanks and praise. Not because He needs this and not because the circumstances we find ourselves in are resolved necessarily the way we would hope. It is because our hearts change when we humbly position ourselves before our King in love and obedience to His will and ways. It is in this place we discover His deep and precious well of joy, which erupts in our hearts as thanks and praise.

In this age of quick Internet access and abundant social media, I wonder if we have wandered off the path of seeking our Savior when our hearts are desperate. Yes, God can use the Internet, and medicine, and all sorts of venues to cure and heal us. But if we haven't sought Him first and waited to hear His reply, then we are simply finding our own answers, developing our own plans, and expecting Him to agree with our decisions. In this scenario He doesn't get the glory, so we don't receive His joy; therefore, our thanks and praise if there is any at all, will not come from humbled hearts full of the awe of God.

There are other God substitutes in our world besides the Internet. Very often we find ourselves turning to family, friends, and even pastors to aid us through trials that were meant to take us first to the Lord.

> *For from Him and through Him and to Him are all things. [For all things originate with Him and come from Him; all things live through Him, and all things center in and tend to consummate and to end in Him.] To Him be glory forever! Amen (so be it).* (Rom 11:36)

He is holy and we have constant access to His holiness, through His Son, Jesus Christ. We enter His presence by faith, and we ask our questions based in trust for what He has done for us and promised us. Even when we are concerned that we may have done something wrong, He is still present, and His greatest desire is to spend a lot of intimate time with us. It is there, in His divine presence, that we will come to know His voice, and we will begin to trust His forgiveness as we learn to repent and realize His faithfulness in washing us clean and making us new. In this sweet place of obedience we will know His glory and receive His joy.

> *Since we have such [glorious] hope (such joyful and confident expectation), we speak very freely and openly and fearlessly. Nor [do we act] like Moses, who put a veil over his face so that the Israelites might not gaze upon the finish of the vanishing [splendor which had been upon it]... But whenever a person turns [in repentance] to the Lord, the veil is stripped off and taken away. Now the Lord is the Spirit, and where the Spirit of the Lord is, there is liberty (emancipation from bondage, freedom). And all of us, as with unveiled face, [because we] continued to behold [in the Word of God] as in a mirror the glory of the Lord, are constantly being transfigured into His very own image in ever increasing splendor and from one degree of glory to another; [for this comes] from the Lord [Who is] the Spirit.* (2 Corinthians 3:12-13, 16-18)

So how does our God get the glory for the things that happen in our lives? He brings us to the point where we have no way of accomplishing the task He has set before us without Him. He takes us beyond what our understanding and skill sets have taught us and reassures us that

Joyfully His

He is God, and His zeal will accomplish it. He told Moses to tell the Pharaoh of Egypt to let the Israelites go. Moses replied to the Lord, "Behold, my own people the Israelites have not listened to me, how then shall Pharaoh give heed to me, who am of deficient and impeded speech?" God responds by repeating His command to Moses to bring His people out of the land of Egypt (Exodus 6:10-13).

We know how this story turns out. God gives Moses god-like powers with which God challenges and defeats every god worshipped in Egypt. This doesn't make Pharaoh listen to Moses at all but instead exposes the intensity of pride and disdain in the king's heart. The struggle between God and the Egyptian king and his idols ends in tragedy for Egypt. The Israelites are freed, and God's will and might are glorified as His people march out into the wilderness in joy.

In a similar way, God's glory manifested joyfully for me when He healed my body from years of abuse and restored my peace. The body that God has given us is a treasure to Him, and while the ideal would be that we keep our bodies in honor and purity, this is not always what happens to us here in our broken world. Thankfully, He is the healer and when we have been born again, our bodies are made new and become the place where He begins to build His sacred temple that houses His Spirit within us.

> *But the person who is united to the Lord becomes one spirit with Him. Shun immorality and all sexual looseness [flee from impurity in thought, word, or deed]. Any other sin which a man commits is one outside the body, but he who commits sexual immorality sins against his own body. Do you not know that your body is the temple (the very sanctuary) of the Holy Spirit Who lives within you, Whom you have received [as a Gift] from God? You are not your own, You were bought with a price [purchased with a preciousness and paid for, made His own]. So then, honor God and bring glory to Him in your body.* (1Corinthians 6: 17-19)

When I was fifteen years old I thought it was probably a good idea to accept Christ as my Savior. I was attending a Christian youth camp and one night we had climbed to the top of a mountain where we sat looking at a gigantic cross. It was lit from the bottom and seemed to me to be the most awesome structure I had ever seen in my life. I remember saying to Jesus as I looked up at that cross, "I believe You, I believe I need this, I WANT this." I don't recall that I ever told anyone else of this decision. We moved to a new state later that year, and I never joined another youth group. The precious seed planted that night fell by the roadside and the birds came and tried to eat it up (Matthew 13) but not before a good, long battle in which Satan aimed to wear me out and steal my soul. God's aim was good, to break me of my pride and self-sufficiency and over throw my independent rebellious heart. God would eventually have victory.

There are many ways that Satan comes into our lives to steal, kill, and destroy. He often will present a hard spiritual battle in our lives and allow us to have what seems like victory only to have us lose our joy. The way he chose to eat up the godly seeds planted in me for salvation was through a prolonged attack on my purity.

I had determined when I asked Jesus into my heart that I would stay pure until I was married. This grew into such an important virtue in my heart that I had been willing to lose boyfriends and even friends that had differing mindsets than I had. By the time we moved to a different state I was already experiencing rejection and punishment from some of my closest friends for my stand on this issue. Finding myself in a new school, isolated from church and with no Christian youth group, I gave up the fight. I don't know if I consciously realized I had begun losing ground, but by the time I turned sixteen—just a little less than a year after moving to our new home—I had been raped. Raped is a complicated term because it wants to produce in our minds a clear-cut picture of two people: one very wicked person and another very victimized person. Sometimes that is clearly the case, but in mine it was not. I do know that, by this time in my life, I had become a sad girl who chose to enter a situation that allowed a young man to take advantage of my intense desire to feel loved and secure. I tried to convince myself for a long time that what had happened to me was okay, and perhaps even love, but it definitely was not. I simply did not have the skills, support, or understanding to stand up for the sanctity of my body any longer. The young man did not have any interest in my honor at all. Once he got what he had been after, I never heard from him again. When a person is used like this, they develop an intense need to control something. In my case, I decided to control my own body by punishing it through bulimia.

Bulimia nervosa is a potentially life-threatening eating disorder. I would eat tons of food and then purge my stomach in unhealthy ways. I was five feet seven inches tall, and in about two years my clothing size went from a healthy size nine to a skeletal size five. The abuse of my body produced a preoccupation in me with my weight and shape. I fell into a pattern of judging myself severely and harshly because I felt so dirty and ugly, which led to bouts of depression and anxiety. I had not really paid attention to my body before, now I just wanted it to go away.

When I was a sophomore in college I was confronted about the bulimia by those who loved me. I adamantly promised I would stop, and I meant it with my whole heart. I was horribly embarrassed and so upset that my behavior had upset anyone. However, anyone reading this who has experienced an eating disorder that has lasted for many years knows I couldn't stop, not on my own, and I didn't. Like the parable of Matthew 13, when the birds eat the seed of Christ, they will stay at it until the seed is completely consumed. Satan wanted no chance of my getting healed, and he would pursue this attack on me all the way into the first years of my marriage.

This pattern of thinking about myself, and my body, was part of what allowed the abuse and destruction that characterized my early relationships. Its poison had only lessened slightly when my first child was born. By the time I was thirty and found myself in the throes of single parenting, the fruit of this poisoned soil produced another crop that would lure me into its dark and battering dungeons once again. That other crop was alcoholism. Not alcoholism by the world's standards, but certainly by God's. By the time I was thirty-two, I knew I had to get back to where I had left off at the age of fifteen. I needed to find Jesus' cross that had beckoned me at that Christian camp so many years before. God showed me a church where I could go, and I began to attend with all my might. This step was the first of many that would lead me on a long road back into the healing arms of Christ.

Abuse and addiction are fruits of a life controlled by Satan's desires and lies. There was a time when the enemy's voice was so familiar and his demons had such control over me, but that time is gone. I know how real and dark the struggles are because I've experienced what they can do, and I've experienced what Christ can do by getting rid of them. Through the power of the Holy Spirit I have been delivered from Satan's grasp and am found firmly planted in the good soil of the heart of Christ. All is to His glory and He gives me such joy!

My body is free, but it does still bear the physical scars from years of abuse. After giving birth to my first child I went on to experience two miscarriages, several surgeries and an erupted tubal pregnancy. By the time I reached my late thirties, my husband and I were diagnosed as infertile; yet, we both felt certain we were supposed to have children. We decided, after years of trying, that we would place it completely in God's hands and let Him decide. God had been very clear with us that other options such as in-vitro were not on the table for us. We had been going to a fertility specialist for a few years, but we had made the choice not to pursue any of his suggestions. We left his office on a warm day in September, and he did not expect to see us back. Over the years we had told him of our faith in Jesus and our trust in His promise that we would have children. Both my husband and I had children from before our marriage, and we rested content that God's plan for more would unfold.

The next few months I remember as an intense struggle. While we were trying to let go of the idea of pregnancy, God appeared to torture us with it. Everywhere we went we were encountering happy pregnant women. I found myself crying out to Him for explanation, and a few months later I came to the realization that our God does not give us desires in our heart in order to torture us, but in order to bring glory to His kingdom. He assured me I was not to stop praying to get pregnant. A few months later, we were indeed pregnant! At five weeks gestation, our doctor hurriedly brought us into his office to examine the placement of the fetus. The danger that the baby would be lodged in my one existing, but heavily damaged fallopian tube was real, and the sooner we knew the better. I will never forget our doctor's reaction when he discovered our son playing around in the uterus right where he belonged. The doctor cried tears of relief and amazement right alongside my husband and me. He looked me in the eye and said, "You keep that faith!" Yes I will! I thank God and I Praise Him, and I give Him the glory. He returns our thanks and praise with boundless joy!

Our son was followed five years later by another precious gift of faith, another son. I was forty-five when my youngest child was born, and I remain thankful every day, as millions of mom's do, for the gift of motherhood. How God chooses to fulfill His promises to us will vary from heart to heart; but one thing remains constant, He is not a man that can lie, He will fulfill in His way and His timing. Stand, sit, or kneel in the faith that holds through the battle and keeps our joy! He will do it.

I have faith that if you believe that you have a God-given desire in your heart for parenthood, He is going to make you a parent in one-way or another. His will is to do good for those who love Him with all their heart, soul, strength, and mind. Lay it completely on His altar, and see what He will do for you. Sarah had to wait until she was ninety-nine years old! Praise God, to Him be the glory!

> *Now Abraham and Sarah were old, well advanced in years; it had ceased to be with Sarah as with [young] women. [She was past the age of childbearing]. Therefore Sarah laughed to herself, saying, After I have become aged shall I have pleasure and delight, my lord (husband), being old also? And the Lord asked Abraham, Why did Sarah laugh, saying, Shall I really bear a child when I am so old? Is anything too hard or too wonderful for the Lord? (Genesis 18:11-14)*

Chapter 5

WISELY HIS

But the wisdom from above is first of all pure (undefiled); then it is peace-loving, courteous (considerate, gentle). [It is willing to] yield to reason, full of compassion and good fruits; it is whole-hearted and straightforward, impartial and unfeigned (free from doubts, wavering, and insincerity). (James 3:17)

Hear the trumpets hear the pipers
One Hundred million angels singin'
Multitudes are marchin' to the big kettledrum
Voices callin', voices cryin'
Some are born and some are dyin'
Its Alpha and Omega's Kingdom come
And the whirlwind is in the thorn tree
The virgins are all trimming their wicks
The whirlwind is in the thorn tree
It's hard for thee to kick against the pricks
Till Armageddon no shalam, no shalom
Then the father hen will call his chickens home
The wise man will bow down before the throne
And at His feet they'll cast their crowns
When the Man comes around
When the Man Comes Around by John R Cash

His Heart Changes Everything

*J*ESUS IS INTERESTED and completely able to meet all our needs, but often His way and timing is different than our own because His will is to change hearts. I desperately needed healing from abuse, and He heard my cry and answered me by teaching me about forgiveness and letting go. Later in my family's life I needed help knowing how to juggle laundry, cooking, and homeschooling. While these things might seem more trivial to us than the cry over infertility, they are just as important to Him. He understands our hearts and sets out to turn our focus away from our trouble to facing Him and coming to trust Him with our all.

He is the one who created us, and He knows how He knit us together in our mother's womb. He understood that I had been relying on my own worldly wisdom to face the growing coldness of my heart. He saw that I believed in His Word that spoke to me of His desire that I be pure in body and spirit and He watched as I had tried in all the human power I could muster up to be victorious in that battle. But I had been focused on the power I thought I was supposed to have in myself. Like the little train in the children's book, I had been taught that all I had to do was *think I can!*[7]

> *His way and timing is different than our own because His will is to change hearts.*

I had used that philosophy "think I can" in many situations before Christ offered me a better way. For example, I discovered that I loved running at some point in my high school career. Facing steep hills, last laps, and long straight-aways all lent well to keeping my mind busy with optimistic ventures. It also kept everyone on the outside distracted by my efforts even while my spirit was in a struggle to survive. I have managed to motivate myself to run all the way up mountains and across long bridges only to find myself on the other side wondering: "What now?" or "Why am I here?" Sure, there is a fair amount of accomplishment and pride in meeting our goals; after

---
[7] Piper, Watty. *The Little Engine that Could.* New York: Platt and Monk. 1930

all, they prove that we can actually do it! A goal achieved is usually just one in a series of steps designed to get you to an even bigger goal, thus we can celebrate each one as worthy of recognition then turn around the next day looking to find a higher hill and a longer bridge to conquer.

Understanding what our goals are and knowing whether they are founded in Christ or the world will ultimately influence the glory we give to God and the joy we have in accomplishing them. I found that while my goals were focused on health, wealth, security, notoriety, comfort, and a host of other things, my joy tended to be short lived and easily overwhelmed by the constant drive to reach the next horizon.

If we are not sure if our goals are of the world or from God, then taking into account how we are acting while we try to reach the goal can tell us a lot. Exhibiting enmity, strife, jealousy, anger, selfishness, drunkenness, carousing, and so on can all weigh-in when our goals are found in the world's wisdom and expectations. These are the fruits of our flesh not the fruit of the Spirit. Fruits of the flesh give glory and power to Satan and can never give God glory or cause our hearts to be in awe in Him. The fruits of the flesh are grown from hearts full of fear of man and love for the world and its systems. They will not result in enduring joy for our hearts or the hearts of those around us.

> *What leads to strife (discord and feuds) and how do conflicts (quarrels and fightings) originate among you? Do they not arise from your sensual desires that are ever warring in your bodily members? You are jealous and covet [what others have] and your desires go unfulfilled; [so] you become murderers. [To hate is to murder as far as your hearts are concerned.] You burn with envy and anger and are not able to obtain [the gratification, the contentment, and the happiness that you seek], so you fight and war. You do not have, because you do not ask. [Or] you do ask [God for them] and yet fail to receive, because you ask with wrong purpose and evil, selfish motives. Your intention is [when you get what you desire] to spend*

> *it in sensual pleasures ... That is why He says, God sets Himself against the proud and haughty, but gives grace [continually] to the lowly (those who are humble enough to receive it). (James 4:1-3, 6b)*

What happens to us when something interrupts our planned goals is another possible gauge of the true motives of our heart and/or the true source of our efforts. Our response will largely depend on whether the goal we are running toward in faith is of our own making or God's. If it is according to our own wisdom, many of us will adopt the "think I can" philosophy and push through cramps, stomachaches, and popping knees in order to win. We might be willing to break promises in relationships or risk broken hearts, even cast aside our morals in order to secure victory. Interruptions to this already stressful venture can then become a source of bitterness, anger, and frustration because they challenge our "think I can" attitude—perhaps even cause it to fail thus stealing the glory and approval we envisioned for ourselves and others. These goals and efforts are not God's; they have become idols of our heart.

> *Lean on, trust in, and be confident in the Lord with all your heart and mind and do not rely on your own insight or understanding. In all your ways know, recognize, and acknowledge Him, and He will direct and make straight and plain your paths. Be not wise in your own eyes; reverently fear and worship the Lord and turn [entirely] away from evil. It shall be health to your nerves and sinews, and marrow and moistening to your bones. (Proverbs 3:5-8)*

This is where I found myself when God, in His mercy, redirected me from holding so tightly to my children. It is a difficult place to find yourself when you know God has given you a promise, but He seems to be taking it away or permitting a delay. My ideas of how God's promises were going to be worked out in my life have often not matched what God has planned. Our choice is clear, we can proudly resist what we are hearing or seeing God do, or we can obey, trust Him, and let go. My heart has been broken in these times but that is exactly what God loves. A broken heart that clings to Jesus lets more of His Spirit in us to shine out.

> *My sacrifice [the sacrifice acceptable] to God is a broken spirit; a broken and a contrite heart such, O God, You will not despise.* (Psalm 51:17)

If our understanding remains the world's understanding, then interruptions loom over us as storms that must be overcome, conquered, or avoided in order to ensure our continued status and glory. If we learn to wisely turn toward God's understanding in our times of trial and storm, then we remain open to Him as He shows us the next step or redirects our way. Following His wisdom in storms and trials will create hope, peace, increased faith and joy as we learn to trust Him completely with our planning and our time.

> *Therefore, since we are justified (acquitted, declared righteous, and given a right standing with God) through faith, let us [grasp the fact that we] have [the peace of reconciliation to hold and to enjoy] peace with God through our Lord Jesus Christ (the Messiah, the Anointed One).* (Romans 5:1)

Do we believe Paul's statement in Romans 5:1 a little or do we believe it a lot? We have all been given a certain amount of faith, and by that amount of faith we step into this relationship with Jesus. He tells us that faith even as small as the size of a mustard seed (that is very small) is enough to move mountains (Matthew 17:20). How can that be so?

In the parable of the mustard seed, Jesus explains that when we take that seed of faith which is given to us and sow it into the fields of our heart, it will grow to be the largest of plants, a tree (Matt 13:31-32). I believe that what He is saying is that if we seek Him and His plan and take the faith we have, however small, and mix that faith into our hearts as we set out to obey Him, then He will grow that faith in our hearts as He shows us His perfect ability to accomplish His will. His zeal will accomplish it, every time (Isaiah 37:32).

If we never seek God's direction for our goals then we won't have His wisdom and our faith will have grown from somewhere or someone else. Our worldly goals and needs require only faith in ourselves. Desires and goals that have come from God will always require faith in God because godly goals will appear almost impossible to accomplish on our own. This is His grace, which gives us the ability of God through the power of the Holy Spirit to accomplish all He asks of us. We receive this free gift of grace when we ask Jesus to be our Savior. As our relationship grows and He becomes the Lord of our lives, we receive more and more grace to step into situations that require more and more faith.

> *Through Him also we have [our] access (entrance, introduction) by faith into this grace (state of God's favor) in which we [firmly and safely] stand. And let us rejoice and exult in our hope of experiencing and enjoying the glory of God.* (Romans 5:2)

Faith is not just something we talk about; it has to be something we act on. Who or what we have faith in is tested and proved by our actions in any given situation, especially hard ones. If we have stepped toward a goal from a sense of competition or out of a desire to please a person rather than out of faith in Christ, then we are putting God to the test and we are sinning (Romans 14:23). Sometimes, out of His heart of grace and mercy, God will allow our unfaithful acts to go unopposed much like a parent may allow a wayward child to go unpunished for a time. However, God will not continue to exert His mercy over our hearts if we continue to neglect His intimacy or refuse to obey His commandments. He is a good parent and will eventually discipline us for our own good because He loves us.

When we step out in faith to obey what we truly believe is a direction from God, we are giving Him the chance to be BIG in our lives. We move toward His direction as He leads in His timing and His way. The hard thing for most of us is taking that first step. We think we have to deserve it or be ready for it. That is our own wisdom and it is faulty. God has given His gifts—forgiveness, mercy, grace, favor, salvation—freely. If we are struggling with our decisions or hesitating to take a step we believe is from God it is probably because we still don't believe He will handle it. We think we have to earn His gifts and somehow deserve them. He simply asks us to receive them. To acknowledge Him means we receive the truth that we can never deserve what He has given us through faith in Jesus Christ. We receive by faith and we act in faith. Jesus paid the price that we could never pay to provide these free gifts for us. If we stay locked in the worldly wisdom of earning and deserving, we will never get what we are after. Satan is never satisfied and will only have to hold out another carrot to frustrate us in our efforts.

Abraham was a man of faith and when God said to go, Abraham picked up his life and went. Abraham never saw the fulfillment of what God had promised him. What kept Abraham from giving up and going back home? The Word tells us it was his faith. He kept pressing on toward God, trusting Him more and more as the journey continued through trials and mistakes. Abraham grew to love and appreciate God more even as he came face to face with his own weaknesses and failures.

> *He will handle it.*

If we don't ever learn to seek God's direction we won't learn to hear the voice of our Lord. If we don't mix what we hear with faith we won't be able to receive what He has promised us. If we don't ever let go of our own works and wisdom and open our hands to be filled with His, we will never see our seed of faith grow. If our seed of faith is never sown into our fields where it can be watered, fertilized, and cultivated, it will never have the opportunity to take root, be strengthened, pruned, and harvested. Our field is our heart, faith in Him allows us to receive His gifts which change our field into His harvest of good works. These good works of faith are evidence of our trust in Him.

Why is this evidence of faith so important? Because it is how we come to be more like Him, bearing His character in our hearts, which is the evidence that Jesus is real and His love is alive. The world is to come to know Him through our love for each other and that love can only grow through act after act of faith.

When John and I had first received the news that we were infertile we responded in faith. When we kept being confronted by happy pregnant couples, we responded first in our own understanding and got angry with God. Feeling tortured by Christ, we wondered why these women were more deserving than ourselves. I remember getting angry and jealous because I really wanted a child so badly. Then I went through a time where I thought that because I had treated my body so badly that I deserved to be infertile. All of this worldly wisdom made me unable to receive the free gift that God had ready for me. I knew what He had promised, but I had to let Him handle it. When I let go of my own efforts and frustrations, He was able to bless us with grace, mercy and more faith.

> *Moreover [let us also be full of joy now!] let us exult and triumph in our troubles and rejoice in our sufferings, knowing that pressure and affliction and hardship produce patient and unswerving endurance. And endurance (fortitude) develops maturity of character (approved faith and tried integrity). And character [of this sort] produces [the habit of] joyful and confident hope of eternal salvation. Such hope never disappoints or deludes or shames us, for God's love has been poured out in our hearts through the Holy Spirit Who has been given to us. (Romans 5:3-5)*

Our household was God designed to test our endurance, joy and hope. I now had five children and I became convinced that I was unable to provide the amount of attention and love they all deserved. I noticed that my love would quickly disappear when they were misbehaving towards each other or me. I decided I needed help to make them behave so that my seemingly limited well would not be tested so severely and used up so quickly. I thought the love I had in my own strength had to be enough and that the problem was their behavior. Pressure, affliction, and hardship weren't producing patience as they pressed against my heart. They were actually making me uncomfortable by revealing impatience, frustration, and anger. My faith was for God to show up, control my environment, and fix the behavior of my kids and family so that I could remain the peaceful and happy person that I believed myself to be. I thought I deserved a peaceful home. God tells us that out of the heart, the mouth speaks (Matthew 15:18); I did not understand yet that what was being pressed out of me was the fruit of my renewed but still deceitful and selfish heart.

Somewhere along the way I learned to go into the closet and pray. I did this fully expecting God to meet my needs by changing my children, husband, and our environment. I could sense God's presence as I sought Him, but as soon as I came out of the closet all the same aggravations were there and the anger and frustration at so little change slowly grew into bitterness. Back in the closet I would go. It felt better in there, separate from all the strife and demands of the world, but it wasn't changing anything. I wasn't seeing the fruit I expected and desired because I was asking selfishly, to appease my own desires. My desires weren't God's desires. I wanted the people in my family, who I believed that I loved, to be the kind of people that were easy to love. It turns out that He had picked all of them especially for me and me for them to show us His glory and to heal our hearts. They didn't need to learn how to behave so I could love them better. We all needed to learn to ask Him for His love, forgiveness, mercy and grace. We needed to ask Him for more and more faith to believe that all He has for us is free through Christ not because we are good, or ever will be. We needed to learn what it meant to receive because all He has for us, whether storm or calm, is good. Then our joy will be full.

> *But seek (aim at and strive after) first of all His kingdom and His righteousness (His way of doing and being right), and then all these things taken together will be given you besides.* (Matthew 6:33)

When our needs seem to go unmet or change appears illusive, God is still at work and He promises to work all things together for the good of those who love Him. He has a protocol for every situation we face, turn to Him and have faith. We must learn from Him to follow His protocol and we must respect that His will is always going to prevail in our lives. We really are wise to want it that way. Only when these truths are firmly planted in our hearts will we see His Glory and experience the joy of His victory.

> *Behold, I stand at the door and knock; if anyone hears and listens to and heeds My voice and opens the door, I will come in to him and will eat with him, and he [will eat] with Me. He who overcomes (is victorious), I will grant him to sit beside Me on My throne, as I Myself overcame (was victorious) and sat down beside My Father on His throne.* (Revelation 3:20-21)

The 'wilderness' is the place where God realigns our will with His. Like the plagues in the Book of Exodus, Egypt—no matter how rich, powerful, and self-sustaining—was going to align with God's will. He had bid His people come into the wilderness and worship "Me". He had asked them to separate themselves from the world that had grown so familiar to them, though it dragged them down and suffered them severely.

> *For the wages which sin pays is death, but the [bountiful] free gift of God is eternal life through (in union with) Jesus Christ our Lord.* (Romans 6:23)

Just as Israel followed Moses out of Egypt and into the desert, we will one day find ourselves in a wilderness-type situation where we learn about the faithfulness of our God. Often wilderness journeys closely follow a spiritual victory or deliverance from some bondage we may have been battling. We respond to these times of newfound freedom with immediate jubilation and joy. This is appropriate and good but we must be aware of what happens next. Like the Israelites, we often find ourselves facing the fact that while we have been victorious, Satan has managed to steal our joy. Tired and thirsty we look into the bitter spring that is our hearts and realize we need healing. This is what happened to the Israelites as they journeyed away from Egypt, crossed the Red Sea, and entered the Wilderness of Shur. Facing our trials and afflictions in God and according to His protocol promises to produce in us the things of the Spirit. Jesus is the only cure for bitter hearts. In His death and resurrection, we can leave behind what we have been and embrace the promise of who we are in Him. As Moses knew to throw the stick into the bitter waters and God made them good to drink, picking up the cross of Christ has the power to turn our bitter hearts to sweet.

> *I will take My children into the Wilderness and there I will speak tenderly to them. I will restore their fruitfulness and turn their valley of trouble into a door of hope.* (Hosea 2:14-15)

Chapter 6

POWERFULLY HIS

*But you shall receive power (ability, efficiency, and might)
when the Holy Spirit has come upon you, and you shall be
My witnesses in Jerusalem and all Judea and Samaria and
to the ends (the very bounds) of the earth. (Act 1:8)*

*The world has lost the power to blush over its vice;
The church has lost her power to weep over it.*[8]

THE SUN HAD just set behind the mountains, and we could hear the rustling of the olive trees as their branches responded to the soft breeze blowing up from the sea. Lazarus was with us at the table, such a miracle to think that he had been dead and buried only a few weeks ago. Now here he was, alive and eating and drinking with us just as he had before! The air was beginning to take on the promising warmth of spring, and we knew Passover was coming. We felt a deep thankfulness to be together with Jesus and were all enjoying the company when Mary came in with a beautiful alabaster jar. She often sat at Jesus' feet so none

---
[8] Ravenhill, Leonard. *Heart Breathings.* Harvey Christian Publishers Inc., 1995 www.harveycp.com.

of us really noticed when she took her normal position there. He smiled at her, and she quietly and reverently broke open the jar that she held so tenderly in her hands. She poured the precious and expensive oil over Jesus' feet. As we watched, she wiped His feet with her hair, and His eyes filled, as they so often did, with love and understanding. The house was filled with the wonderful fragrance of perfume.

Our hearts were still wondering about the sweetness of that night as we talked among ourselves about what we had seen and heard since. Six days after Mary anointed Jesus' feet we had traveled to Jerusalem with Him to celebrate Passover. We were supposed to eat a lamb, a perfect lamb without blemish or spot. Jesus, dressed in an apron began the evening by washing each our feet. This practice was not unusual but who was doing the washing surprised us all. Normally the washing of our very dirty feet would have been carried out by a servant or even one of us. Here was Jesus, our beloved teacher, bending down to serve us. There had been so much to take in and try to understand. Jesus told us that He had eagerly desired to share this Passover supper with us and we too were anticipating the joy of eating the Passover meal with Him. This night was special for us all and yet He did not eat the bread or drink the wine that He offered to us. He told us about the bread we were eating. He revealed to us that it was His body and that the wine was His blood. Some of us were disarmed and a few confused.

The next twenty-four hours became a blur as one unexpected turn followed another. One of our fellow disciples betrayed the location of our Master to the authorities. While we were supposed to be praying in the Garden of Gethsemane on the Mount of Olives, soldiers came and took Jesus away. Our emotions moved from disarmed to helpless and even scared as we watch Him be arrested and taken into custody.

The following morning, we watch in horror as Jesus was placed on a cross and cursed. When the lambs were killed at twilight, some of us were there to hear Jesus takes His last breath, crying out to God, "It is finished!" Others

Powerfully His

of us had fled, fearing for our lives and ashamed of our cowardly hearts. An earthquake shook the entire city as Jesus died and we found out quickly that the curtain in the Temple had ripped from top to bottom. Jesus was lowered from the cross and they buried Him in a rich man's tomb and we all went home wondering what had happened. As our families were eating their Passover meals it was more somber than usual. Remembering our deliverance from Egypt and Pharaoh was now enhanced by the memory of our last hours with Jesus, eating the bread and drinking the cup of what He had called His body and His blood, the New Covenant. What could this mean?

A fear began to flicker in some of us as the dark hours of the morning brought the Sabbath of Unleavened Bread. There was no work to be done today and we began to feel unsettled. Those of us that stayed in Jerusalem hid and felt lost, confused, and alone. We thought this was going to turn out so differently. We thought our Master was the hoped for Messiah, the Savior, Hosanna! We believed He had come to set our people free from the oppression of Rome.

Then came the most glorious miracle of all. On the first day of the week, Sunday, after three days and three nights in the tomb, we hear our master is alive! He is risen! We see Him, and Thomas is invited to touch His wounds. He is real. The next forty days He is with us again almost like before. He walks with us, eats supper with us, and we break bread like we did at the Last Supper we had shared together. We begin to piece together in our hearts the puzzle of who our Teacher really is. We begin to understand more clearly what God's amazing plan really was. He has set us free, not the way we expected, but even better than we could have dreamed.

> *Then He [thoroughly] opened up their minds to understand the Scriptures, And said to them, Thus it is written that the Christ (the Messiah) should suffer and on the third day rise from (among) the dead, And that repentance [with a view to and as the condition of] forgiveness of sins should be preached in His name to all nations, beginning from Jerusalem. You*

> *are witnesses of these things. And behold, I will send forth upon you what My Father has promised; but remain in the city [Jerusalem] until you are clothed with power from on high.* (Luke 24:45-48)

> *For John baptized with water, but not many days from now you shall be baptized with (placed in, introduced into) the Holy Spirit.* (Act 1:5)

Jesus had instructed us to remain in Jerusalem. He told us that the time had come for His return to the Father. He assured us that He must go in order for us to receive the gift of the Holy Spirit. He promised us that He would be making a place for us in His Father's house. We are to wait for the gift we have been promised from God our Father in heaven. With this power we are to go and be His witnesses in Jerusalem and all Judea, Samaria, and the ends of the earth. He is caught up into the clouds and is so quickly out of our sight. We watch, perhaps we are all hoping for another glimpse of Him. Two angels inform us that He will, one day, come back the same way He left. Until then, we are to go and obey.

The biblical feast of Pentecost is fast approaching and we join the throng of pilgrims making their way into Jerusalem to celebrate. This appointed time in Hebrew is called Shavuot. None of us feel particularly like celebrating. Our fellow pilgrims are looking forward to God's promise of His presence at Shavuot in their flimsily built, roofless sukkas. We are longing for His presence with us like we had with Him only ten days before today. Had we appreciated it while we had it? There are so many questions that seem unanswered. Things we wished we had asked or that we had listened better to when He was with us. We had much to think and pray about as we entered the upper room that was still full of memories of that last supper with our Master.

In the city of Jerusalem and its surrounding area, families are gathering and remembering Exodus 19. They are intent on worshipping God and celebrating the Law, which had been given to them on Mt. Sinai. All of the disciples are in the upper room, waiting and praying.

The third morning there were thunders and lightings, and a thick cloud upon the mountain, and a very loud trumpet blast, so that all the people in the camp trembled. Then Moses brought the people from the camp to meet God, and they stood at the foot of the mountain. Mount Sinai was wrapped in smoke, for the Lord descended upon it in fire; its smoke ascended like that of a furnace, and the whole mountain quaked greatly. As the trumpet blast grew louder and louder, Moses spoke and God answered him with a voice. The Lord came down upon Mount Sinai to the top of the mountain, and the Lord called Moses to the top of the mountain, and Moses went up. (Exodus 19:16-20)

The people gathering in Jerusalem that year were all thoroughly schooled about Mt. Sinai. They had been told the story all of their lives. They knew with keen observation that even if they would dare to touch the mountain, they would die. Moses had been able to ascend the mountain and receive the Law, but they were not Moses. He had stayed in the mists of the mountain for forty days—too long for some of their ancestors to stay faithful to a God or leader who were both so new to their understanding. Their lack of courage and faith led them to take a tragic turn from the mountain and from God.[9]

When Moses was told to go down from the mountain to begin sharing the gift of the Torah with God's people, he found a rebellious people. In His forty day absence, the Israelites had lost sight and hope in a God who had delivered them from oppressors and led them lovingly through the wilderness. They had turned away from the holiness of Sinai and back to the idols of their captors and slave masters. Moses was met with loud celebrations of a people accustomed to the worship of a golden calf idol.

For I am zealous for you with a godly eagerness and a divine jealousy, for I have betrothed you to one Husband, to present you as a

---

[9] The Torah or the Law, which in its entirety, would eventually encompass the first five books of the Bible and was be given by God to the Israelites through Moses until the second generation of free Israelites entered Canaan. At this conjecture Moses would have been carrying the two tablets of stone containing the Ten Commandments which was to be a physical sign of the Mosaic Covenant between God and His people.

> *chaste virgin to Christ. [Hos. 2:19, 20.] But [now] I am fearful, lest that even as the serpent beguiled Eve by his cunning, so your minds may be corrupted and seduced from wholehearted and sincere and pure devotion to Christ.* (2Corinthians 11:2-3)

These were the words spoken a few years later by the Apostle Paul and they are a good reminder to all of us of Jesus' love for us and how we need to stand watchful over our own hearts. We are so quickly deceived by what is familiar to us. We must be zealous for our Lord and Savior, Jesus Christ. Prepared in our hearts as a bride prepares to become a wife to her bridegroom.

Aaron, perhaps lured by the idea of pleasing the people, agreed to make a golden calf so they could worship it. Having lived his life in Egypt amidst this people, Aaron was familiar with the Egyptian gods. His familiarity was a snare to him. When Moses took longer than expected the people began to turn back to their own mindsets. The Egyptian panoply of gods and traditions gave the group many wrong paths to choose from. The Israelites picked the calf (Exodus 3:21), and Aaron fashioned it for them.

Moses was a true leader with the heart of the Father. He went directly to the one he had left in charge and to whom he had given his authority. Moses asked Aaron, "What did these people do to you that you have brought so great a sin upon them?" Aaron, like all of us caught in sin, was tempted to pass the blame and he did, pointing out the evilness of the people instead of recognizing the deceitfulness of his own heart.

> *Then Moses stood in the gate of the camp, and said, whoever is on the Lord's side, let him come to me. And all the Levites [the priestly tribe] gathered together to him. And he said to them, Thus says the Lord God of Israel, Every man put his sword on his side and go in and out from gate to gate throughout the camp and slay every man his brother, and every man his companion, and every man his neighbor. And the sons of Levi did according to the word of Moses; and there fell of the people that day about 3000 men.* (Exodus 32:26-28)

Three thousand of the Levitical priests, sons and daughters, mothers and wives, died that day because they would not turn from their wrong perspectives in order to come to God's truth. God gave them a choice to turn around, to change their way of thinking, but they would not. Instead they sinned and died. God has always said that sin is death.

> And Moses said [to the Levites, By your obedience to God's command] you have consecrated yourselves today [as priests] to the Lord, each man [at the cost of being] against his own son and his own brother, that the Lord may restore and bestow His blessing upon you this day. (Exodus 32:29)

This is the cross that Jesus says we must bear in order to be a part of Him. Moses and the Levitical priests bore it here in Exodus. Abraham bore it on the day he led Isaac up the mountain with a willingness and faith to sacrifice his only son. He believed that God would still make good on His promise that Isaac was the promised seed from Abraham and Sarah. Rahab bore it when she hid the spies and helped them escape. We bear it every time we step out in faith to do the will of God against our own will and against our own mindsets. This is one way mindsets change. It's how we get a new perspective and heart that is like His.

The Good News of Jesus allows us to turn from the fearful views of Mt. Sinai and face in a very different direction. This new perspective reveals an even better mountain. The Word tells us to look toward Mt. Zion.

> Look upon Zion, the city of our set feasts and solemnities! Your eyes shall see Jerusalem, a quiet habitation, a tent that shall not be taken down; not one of its stakes shall ever be pulled up, neither shall any of its cords be broken. But there the Lord will be for us in majesty and splendor a place of broad rivers and streams, where no oar-propelled boat can go, and no mighty and stately ship can pass. For the Lord is our Judge, the Lord is our Lawgiver, the Lord is our King; He will save us. (Isaiah 33:20-22)

When the disciples watched Jesus die on the cross that Passover day two thousand years ago, they were likely still very much aware of Mt. Sinai. In its shadow, which made the people fear, they denied Him, gave up hope, and fled. They hid from the curse they were sure would follow after them as it seemed to have followed Jesus. It was just a shadow, however; the truth would be revealed three days and three nights later.

Our false mindsets can make us run and hide. Wrong thinking can convince us to be afraid. It can keep us locked in cages of tradition and culture that can say to us, "you cannot", "you will not", "you never will be", and in agreement with them we run right back to those familiar enemies. We are sure they will give us security and restore our sense of control and power. What we can come to realize, however, is that familiar does not equate to being secure. Feeling secure or good doesn't mean we are in God's divine will for our lives. We have a tendency to demand our rights in order to access what pleases us. We do this so we can have the power we believe we need. This kind of selfish grab is rooted in pleasing us and other people. We like feeling we are in control and have the power to make others or ourselves happy.

Jesus' disciples had earlier quibbled about power as they walked together. They discussed who would be seated next to Him when He came to His throne. They imagined in those seats they would have the security and power they had always dreamed of. Jesus, knowing the horrific cup He must drink at His crucifixion replied so humbly to their innocent aspirations.

> *And James and John, the sons of Zebedee, approached Him and said to Him, Teacher, we desire You to do for us whatever we ask of You. And He replied to them, What do you desire Me to do for you? And they said to Him, Grant that we may sit, one at Your right hand and one at [Your] left hand, in Your glory (Your majesty and splendor). But Jesus said to them, You do not know what you are asking. Are you able to drink the cup that I drink or be baptized with the baptism [of affliction] with which I am baptized? And they replied to Him, We are able. And*

Jesus told them, The cup that I drink you will drink, and you will be baptized with the baptism with which I am baptized, But to sit at My right hand or at My left hand is not Mine to give; but [it will be given to those] for whom it is ordained and prepared. (Mark 10:35-40)

These two, James and John, would drink of the cup of affliction and would be with Him where He is because of their love for Him. They would not be joining Him on either side on the particular day Jesus was warning them about just a verse before this one. Jesus had just spoken to them of His coming crucifixion. On that day there would be two that joined in His cup of affliction but for very different reasons and with very different hearts. James and John hoped to prove the integrity of heart to bear the cross for the Gospel even unto death. In contrast, it would be two thieves that joined Jesus in His affliction as He died for our sins on the cross. One to the right and the other to the left of Him. One recognizing the real power of God, the other determined to exert his prideful justifications to the bitter end (Luke 23:39-43). Foolishly the one missed his last chance for redemption by choosing to join the crowd in mocking the Son of God. Our hearts are so deceitful.

> *The two robbers were no different in sin, but crucially different in heart.*

We would be wise perhaps to remember we are really all thieves and murderers in dire need of a Savior. The two robbers were no different in sin, but crucially different in heart. The heart of repentance showed true in the other man because he:

- Respected God (do you not even fear God)
- Knew his own sin (under the same condemnation...we indeed justly)
- Knew Jesus (this man has done nothing wrong)

- Called out to Jesus as Lord (he said, Jesus, Lord)
- Believed Jesus (remember me when you come into Your kingdom)

The man's heart was sincere; we know that because Jesus assures him that he would join Him in paradise that very day. Jesus fulfills the Law, and through His love we can also. All other power and sources of security apart from Jesus will lead us to death. His way is the only way if we want to live life and live it more abundantly.

When the disciples walked up the stairs into the upper room forty days after Jesus' resurrection they may not have known it yet, but they had accomplished a Victory. With every "Yes, I love you Lord," that Peter spoke, with every one of them agreeing to go to Jerusalem and wait and pray, each step turned them from a focus on Mt. Sinai and its law toward a fulfilled law of love to be found in a gaze fixed on Mt. Zion. It is here on Mt. Zion that God will again send His Son and make all things New.

> THEN I saw a new sky (heaven) and a new earth, for the former sky and the former earth had passed away (vanished), and there no longer existed any sea. And I saw the holy city, the new Jerusalem, descending out of heaven from God, all arrayed like a bride beautified and adorned for her husband; (Revelation 21:1-2 and Isaiah 65:17)

It had not been an easy path. It had been rocky and confusing at times; but in Him, the disciples had accomplished it. They had kept the faith. They were about to embrace the real and true power of God. They were also about to enter into the most trying time of their lives, ministering the Good News of Christ to the world.

> A Song of Ascents. Those who trust in, lean on, and confidently hope in the Lord are like Mount Zion, which cannot be moved but abides and stands fast forever. As the mountains are round about

Jerusalem, so the Lord is round about His people from this time forth and forever. (Psalm 125:1-2)

These men and women had submitted their lives to Jesus in such astonishing ways. Knowing little of what awaited them, many had left homes, families, and jobs to follow Jesus. They had changed their direction radically in order to do something so completely new. Do we grasp this type of submission? Even now, after Jesus had been crucified, died, buried, and resurrected, they were willing to come together in Jerusalem where they might all be arrested. There was a very real chance that the authorities in the city wanted very much to kill all of Jesus' followers. They refused to submit to their fears and instead submitted to the authority of their risen Lord, Jesus Christ. Even unto death. That is radical submission.

Don't be afraid of what you are about to suffer. The devil will throw some of you into prison to test you. You will suffer for ten days. But if you remain faithful even when facing death, I will give you the crown of life. (Revelation 2:10)

According to Webster's 1828 dictionary, *submission* is the act of yielding or surrendering power or authority to the control or government of another without murmuring; to give up resistance.[10] Many of the disciples' fellow Jews were resisting any change to the covenant they had been raised to love and understand. The celebration of this covenant was the reason so many Jews were in Jerusalem. The disciples themselves may have been thinking and praying about all the things they had learned as children from the Exodus and Moses to the Passover. They had witnessed their Lord become the perfect sacrificial lamb and had been witnesses to His resurrection. They may have been pondering all that Jesus had taught them, especially perhaps over the past forty days

---
10 Webster, Noah. First Edition of An American Dictionary of the English Language. G&C Merriam Company permission to reprint 1828 edition. 1967 & 1995 by the Foundation for American Christian Education, Chesapeake, VA. *Submit.*

since He was resurrected. He was truly alive; they knew that, it was a fact. There is a good chance they were still wanting more understanding about what this all meant for them.

> *Behold, the days are coming, says the Lord, when I will make a new covenant with the house of Israel and with the house of Judah, Not according to the covenant which I made with their fathers in the day when I took them by the hand to bring them out of the land of Egypt, My covenant which they broke, although I was their Husband, says the Lord. But this is the covenant which I will make with the house of Israel: After those days, says the Lord, I will put My law within them, and on their hearts will I write it; and I will be their God, and they will be My people… For I will forgive their iniquity, and I will [seriously] remember their sin no more. (Jeremiah 31:31-34)*

Jewish families had longed for this new covenant spoken of by the prophets. The disciples knew Jesus had said He came to fulfill the law and the prophets. They must have been so thankful to be together in the upper room to pray and to wait. Israel had been hoping for this promise to be fulfilled for fifteen hundred years. Even Job spoke of this longing.

> *Whatever happens, I will be found guilty. So what's the use of trying? Even if I were to wash myself with soap and clean my hands with lye, You would plunge me into a muddy ditch, and my own filthy clothing would hate me. "God is not a mortal like me, so I cannot argue with Him or take Him to trial. If only there were a mediator between us, someone who could bring us together. The mediator could make God stop beating me, and I would no longer live in terror of His punishment. Then I could speak to Him without fear, but I cannot do that in my own strength. (Job 9:29-35 NLT)*

Ten days after the disciples walked up the steps to the upper room, fifty days since Jesus was resurrected, Pentecost arrives. Suddenly the room changes and the baptism Jesus promised begins. There is a sound from heaven like a roaring windstorm and it fills their ears and heads and the whole house is consumed by its power. They look at each other to see if it's just them hearing this, and then they see flames like tongues of fire settling down on each of their heads. They feel His power envelope them, and it soaks them until their whole being is full of His Spirit. They begin speaking in other languages, as the Holy Spirit leads them.

> *"And now I will send the Holy Spirit, just as My Father promised. But stay here in the city until the Holy Spirit comes and fills you with power from heaven".* (Luke 24:49, NLT)

They can't stay still in this power. They feel urged to move toward the windows where they keep speaking in this new tongue. The power in them feels like lightning and thunder but it doesn't hurt, instead it emboldens them and lifts up their eyes and their voices. It speaks words out of their mouths they don't recognize as their own. They are in awe! (Acts 2:1-4 personal paraphrase)

> *At that time there were devout Jews from every nation living in Jerusalem. When they heard the loud noise, everyone came running, and they were bewildered to hear their own languages being spoken by the believers. They were completely amazed. "How can this be?" they exclaimed. "These people are all from Galilee, and yet we hear them speaking in our own native languages! Here we are—Parthians, Medes, Elamites, people from Mesopotamia, Judea, Cappadocia, Pontus, the province of Asia, Phrygia, Pamphylia, Egypt, and the areas of Libya around Cyrene, visitors from Rome (both Jews and converts to Judaism), Cretans, and Arabs. And we all hear these people speaking in our own languages about the wonderful things God has done!" They stood there amazed and perplexed. "What can this mean?" they asked each other.* (Acts 2:5-12)

Even as some scoffers accuse the disciples of being drunk, Peter, in the power now of the Holy Spirit, stands and opens his mouth. The boldness and courage of the truth of the Gospel pours out to the awed crowds in Jerusalem. Peter tells them the story of the Gospel of Christ and their part in crucifying their Lord and Savior. Peter has the power of Christ, and the people are pierced to their hearts. They say to him, "what should we do?" Peter replies;

> *Each of you must repent of your sins and turn to God, and be baptized in the name of Jesus Christ for the forgiveness of your sins. Then you will receive the gift of the Holy Spirit. This promise is to you, and to your children, and even to the Gentiles—all who have been called by the Lord our God." Then Peter continued preaching for a long time, strongly urging all his listeners, "Save yourselves from this crooked generation!" Those who believed what Peter said were baptized and added to the church that day—about 3,000 in all.* (Acts 2:38-41)

See that number three thousand? Our God not only redeems us to Himself. He not only provides us with power from on High, but He also loves to restore. He restored to Himself the same number of souls that were lost at Mt. Sinai. He is so good!

> *Be glad then, you children of Zion, and rejoice in the Lord, your God; for He gives you the former or early rain in just measure and in righteousness, and He causes to come down for you the rain, the former rain and the latter rain, as before. And the [threshing] floors shall be full of grain and the vats shall overflow with juice [of the grape] and oil. And I will restore or replace for you the years that the locust has eaten—the hopping locust, the stripping locust, and the crawling locust, My great army which I sent among you. And you shall eat in plenty and be satisfied and praise the name of the Lord, your God, Who has dealt wondrously with you. And My people*

> *shall never be put to shame. And you shall know, understand, and realize that I am in the midst of Israel and that I the Lord am your God and there is none else. My people shall never be put to shame. And afterward I will pour out My Spirit upon all flesh; and your sons and your daughters shall prophesy, your old men shall dream dreams, your young men shall see visions. Even upon the menservants and upon the maidservants in those days will I pour out My Spirit.* (Joel 2:23-29)

Our God wants to restore us to Himself just like He restored to Himself the three thousand Jews on the day of Pentecost. If you haven't invited the Savior to be yours, if you haven't invited Him into your life to rule and reign, let today be the day. If you haven't had a baptism of the Holy Spirit, it is for you. Look at verse 39 in Acts 2 again. It says that the promise of the Holy Spirit is for us who have repented of our sins, turned to God, and been baptized in the name of Jesus Christ. It is for you today if you will have Him. He says it is also for our children and for all the world. This is where the real power lies, in our giving up our all to be totally surrendered to Him.

> *For I am not ashamed of the Gospel (good news) of Christ, for it is God's power working unto salvation [for deliverance from eternal death] to everyone who believes with a personal trust and a confident surrender and firm reliance, to the Jew first and also to the Greek, For in the Gospel a righteousness which God ascribes is revealed, both springing from faith and leading to faith [disclosed through the way of faith that arouses to more faith]. As it is written, The man who through faith is just and upright shall live and shall live by faith.*
> (Romans 1:16-17)

Chapter 7

MERCIFULLY HIS

He has shown you, O man, what is good; And what does the LORD require of you but to do justly, to love mercy, and to walk humbly with your God
(MICAH 6:8, NKJ)

The Lights of the House, the shouts of the children, the lullaby that my wife was softly cooing, the occasional yips of Jack—all faded as I walked under the velvet sky into the woods. Its paths I knew as well as the road down the valley and into the village. But this one night I missed the straightway and turned onto a path I had not seen before. The branches that laced across it closed behind me as I stumbled on jutting roots and rocks, until soon there was no path to follow. So I sat and waited for the moon to rise and light my way home. But instead of the moon, thunderheads came up and winked out the stars one by one. I knew fear, yet I slept.

Listen to the dream that I dreamed that night in the wilderness of the world.[11]

---

11 Bunyan, John. *Pilgrim's Progress. As Retold by Gary D. Schmidt.* William B. Eerdmans Pub Co., Grand Rapids, Michigan. 1994. *Introduction.* (Used with Permission).

*G*od's wilderness is described by the Hebrew word *midbar,* and it defines God's wilderness as a place of desert, open field, uncultivated, dry and uninhabited space.[12] In contrast, Jerusalem is described as a plateau surrounded by a rich and fertile valley where we will experience spiritual richness and God's abundant provision. Babylon, on the other hand is a wilderness of the world, barren spiritually and dangerous physically as it is abundant in the provisions, temptations and, dainties of the enemy of our souls. God Himself asks if He has been a wilderness to Israel in Jeremiah 2:31-32. Have I been a wilderness to you Israel? A land of darkness, like a way without light? Have I been like a land without food? In the next verse He asks why do my people say we have broken loose, and we are free to roam at large and don't have to answer to you anymore? God acknowledges that Israel, His people, His bride has forgotten she is engaged and covenanted to be married. The Bible also shares that God can make us as a wilderness too.

> *Plead with your mother [your nation]; plead, for she is not My wife and I am not her Husband; [plead] that she put away her [marks of] harlotry from her face and her adulteries from between her breasts, Lest I strip her naked and make her as in the day she was born, and make her as a wilderness and set her like a parched land and slay her with thirst. (Hosea 2:2-3)*

Webster's 1828 Dictionary describes the word *wilderness* as a desert; a tract of land or region uncultivated and uninhabited by human beings, whether a forest or a wide barren plain.[13] In the United States, we might think of the wilderness in terms of forests and vast mountainous expanses where few, if any, people live. I tend to picture the Negev desert in Israel, which is a large tract of dry, desert land south of Jerusalem, between the Sinai Peninsula and Jordan River.

---

12 The Complete Word Study: Old Testament. King James Version. Zodhiates, Siros, Th. D. AMG Publishers Chattanooga, TN 37422, USA.1994.The Hebrew and Chaldee Dictionary.P.61. #4057 *Midbar.*
13 Webster, Noah. American Dictionary of the English Language. 1967 reprint of 1828 edition. Foundation for American Christian Education. *Wilderness.*

When I was a little girl in France, wandering around the gardens near our apartments I discovered my own personal wilderness of Cactus and Palm Trees. These provided me with hours of adventures as I followed Mediterranean snails making iridescent trails that I imagined were just for me. I would disappear into these well-manicured, completely desolate gardens for hours during the day. Here it didn't matter that I didn't speak the language or understand the culture of the city I lived in. I fell in love with this place in its wilderness of thorny cactus flowers and snail trails.

After France and living in New Jersey, it was salamanders and long hours spent building little homes for them under the rocks in the woods. Later, I found I loved the rigor of climbing around clefts of rocks in the Allegheny Mountains. I would alight from the woods onto the tops of mountains and see the vastness before me. In that place of utter aloneness something indescribably peaceful would fill me. I would return home more energized and accompanied with a refreshingly humble perspective on my place in this world.

The wilderness can change quickly and without much warning. Faced with an approaching storm or cold front, the vastness can change from a place of fulfillment to a place of real danger and fear. I remember camping with our kids when they were relatively young in the Big Horn Mountains of Wyoming. We had borrowed a pop up camper and left home in early June. The climb to our camping spot was over ten thousand feet, and what had been a seventy-degree day at the bottom turned into high thirties with snow at the top. Night time found us shivering in our camper and using socks to warm our hands. We had failed to remember our geography and didn't pack or prepare for the unexpected temperature changes.

It is in the extremes of this place called the wilderness that we are able to see the truth that can lay hidden in the deeper recesses of our hearts. When forced to change or adapt to wilderness afflictions, sometimes what we have to face in our hearts is anything but holy. It is God's mercy that chooses to reveal these weaknesses so we have the opportunity to deal with them. These places where we resist the changes necessary in any given situation are the places in our hearts that still don't want to submit. These are areas in our heart that could be susceptible to sin and therefore are vulnerable to the enemy who wants to stop us in our walk with Jesus or at least block our ability to fulfill our call.

> *And when the devil had ended every [the complete cycle of] temptation, he [temporarily] left Him [that is, stood off from Him] until another more opportune and favorable time. Then Jesus went back full of and under the power of the [Holy] Spirit into Galilee, and the fame of Him spread through the whole region round about.* (Luke 4:13-14)

Jesus' time in the wilderness can be referred to as a complete cycle of temptation. In the Amplified Bible, a complete cycle is used to describe a period of time where Jesus was attacked with every temptation. Jesus suffered through these afflictions from Satan without fear, and He came out of the wilderness full of and under the power of the Spirit of God (Luke 4:1). Praise God, in Him, we can too.

The word *wilderness* in Greek is *eremos* and means lonesome, wasteland, desert, solitary.[14] Jesus went into this land, alone and for forty days was tempted by the devil in every way. It is clear from that description that during the entire time there were many temptations. It is reassuring to us that our Savior experienced all the temptations that we will face and He did it without sinning. He is able to give us the wisdom and discernment we need to battle our own wilderness journey's if we will ask Him, hear His voice, and obey. The devil appears to have saved three specific types of temptation for the end of Jesus' journey, and the Word shares more detail about these than the many others. We read that when the forty days of trial in the wilderness were ended, Jesus hungered (Luke 4, Matthew 4, Mark 1: 12-13).

---

[14] The Complete Word Study: New Testament. King James Version. Zodhiates, Spiros, Th.D. AMG Publishers Chattanooga, TN 37422, USA. 1991. The Greek Dictionary of the New Testament. P.32. #2048 *Eremos*.

Jesus' Three Temptations

1. **Lust of the Flesh:** The Lord was hungry and the devil tempts Jesus to turn a stone into bread so He could eat.

2. **Lust of the Eyes:** Jesus could have quickly been recognized as the Messiah by taking up the devil on his offer to escape from the suffering and just skip to ruling the world. Satan had been given that power (Ephesians 2:2) and now offered it to our Lord in return for His allegiance to Satan.

3. **Pride of Life:** Satan tempts Jesus to prove who He says He is by challenging Him to jump from the pinnacle of the Temple. The devil uses a quote from Psalm 91 in his challenge.

The order of the temptations is not what I believe is important and each gospel shares the same temptations but in slightly different order. What I think is important is how Jesus responded to each one.

1. Lust of the Flesh: Jesus responds with "man does not live by bread only, but man lives by every word that proceeds out of the mouth of the Lord."

This comes from Deuteronomy 8:3 and reminds us how God humbled the Israelites and allowed them to go hungry in the wilderness so that He could show them He was faithful and able to supply them with manna in the wilderness. It was His mercy that allowed their hunger so they would come to know His promise of provision. This is not speaking just of physical food, but also spiritual. When we limit our spiritual food to only Him, we have the opportunity to discover what Jesus means when He says that He is the bread of life, and that if we come to Him we will never be hungry again (John 6:35).

2. Lust of the Eyes: Jesus tells the devil, "Be gone Satan, for it is written, thou shall worship the Lord thy God, and Him only shall thou serve."

In Deuteronomy 6:12, Moses warns the people to beware of the temptation to take God's provision for granted and forget it is He who gives us all that is good in our lives. It is a warning for us as well that we will be tempted, perhaps especially in times of plenty and peace, to forget who delivered us from our bondage and provided us with our talents and gifting.

> *You shall [reverently] fear the Lord your God and serve Him and swear by His name [and presence]. You shall not go after other gods, any of the gods of the peoples who are round about you; For the Lord your God in the midst of you is a jealous God; lest the anger of the Lord your God be kindled against you, and He destroy you from the face of the earth. (Deuteronomy 6:13-15)*

During times of peace, we can be tempted to compromise our attention and affection by turning to distractions and giving other gods the glory only He deserves.

3. The Pride of Life: Jesus reminds Satan that we are not to tempt the Lord our God.

> *You shall not tempt and try the Lord your God as you tempted and tried Him in Massah. (Deuteronomy 6:16)*

What happened at Massah? This was when the Israelites had moved into the Wilderness of Sin and encamped at Rephidim, but there was no water for the people to drink. The frustration began to build again toward Moses. The Israelites were afraid that they might die in the wilderness. In the wilderness journeys of God our hearts will be proven and tested. The trials we encounter will prove our need for God's intervention. Our hearts will reveal their faithfulness or their doubts and fears. Will we trust in Him to do what He has promised He will do?

If doubt and fear overtake our faith, and we come to the conclusion that God has abandoned us, we test God. When we perceive that our expectations have not been met the way we believed God should meet them, how do we react? We can accept, trust, and submit to the unexpected or be tempted to doubt and resist. There are acceptable times to test God, like Gideon tested Him to make sure he, Gideon, understood God's will. It is unacceptable to God that we have hearts full of fear rooted in doubt. He wants and is able to change our fears and doubts to faith and confidence. Will we trust Him to do it?

> *Therefore, the people contended with Moses, and said, Give us water that we may drink. And Moses said to them, Why do you find fault with me? Why do you tempt the Lord and try His patience? But the people thirsted there for water, and the people murmured against Moses, and said, Why did you bring us up out of Egypt to kill us and our children and livestock with thirst? So Moses cried to the Lord, What shall I do with this people? ... and the Lord said ... you shall strike the rock, and water shall come out of it, that the people may drink. And Moses did so in the sight of the elders of Israel. He called the place Massah [proof] and Meribah [contention] because of the faultfinding of the Israelites and because they tempted and tried the patience of the Lord, saying, Is the Lord among us or not.* (Exodus 17: 2-7)

I was in the New Jersey wilderness at the age of nine camping with a group I thought were my friends, and I saw what was in my heart. I became frustrated because I had to walk through the dark woods to go to the bathroom. Then I experienced the consequences of overeating sweets that others and I had brought. I didn't take responsibility for these choices however. Instead I chose to resent the leadership that had allowed us to eat too much and then sent us to bed. I solved my discomfort by calling my earthly dad and he came and got me. I effectually abandoned ship on one of my first wilderness journeys.

Our heavenly Father, in His divine mercy, doesn't always choose that same route. Now that I'm grown and born again into Jesus I cry out to my Father in Heaven, and He answers me. How He answers me is in His mercy and doesn't always include the quick escape that I would like.

> *The LORD is near to all who call on him, to all who call on him in truth. He fulfills the desire of those who fear him; he also hears their cry and saves them.* (Psalm 145:18-19)

God's mercy in the wilderness spared Miriam from a heart resistant to God's chosen authority. God saved her by giving her leprosy. This trial started when Miriam and Aaron decided together to confront Moses. Miriam was the sister of Moses and Aaron and we can't be completely sure why they chose to confront their brother, but perhaps it had to do with Moses' decision to give over authority to the 70 elders (Numbers 11). This could have had the effect of overshadowing Miriam and Aaron and taken away from their own distinctive role, power or authority. In any case, Miriam and Aaron challenged their brother's leadership decisions. The Bible says, "God heard them," and He loved Moses whom He had chosen. Aaron and Miriam came into agreement with each other against God's chosen leader. It was Miriam and Aaron attacking Moses, but it was Miriam who was struck with leprosy by God.

> *And the anger of the Lord was kindled against them, and He departed. And when the cloud departed from over the Tent, behold, Miriam was leprous, as white as snow. And Aaron looked at Miriam, and, behold, she was leprous! And Aaron said to Moses, Oh, my lord, I plead with you, lay not the sin upon us in which we have done foolishly and in which we have sinned. Let her not be as one dead, already*

> *half decomposed when he comes out of his mother's womb.* (Numbers 12:9-12)

We might be asking ourselves, "How is this God's mercy?" I think this is an example of using proximity to power to vent a perceived wrong. I think this was personal and familial. Miriam was attacking Moses because she and Aaron thought they were entitled to address Moses on this level perhaps because they were his closest blood relatives.

God makes it clear in the law that His chosen leaders are His and are to be served and respected whether we agree with their decisions or not. It serves us well to remember that it is very dangerous to attack God's leaders even if we are right in our concerns about their leadership choices. Aaron and Miriam both attacked, yet it was only Miriam who was given leprosy. Aaron was spared this time, and his heart quickly sought mercy for his sister from Moses. Perhaps this mercy in his heart had been planted there when God had shown Aaron mercy over the golden calf issue at Mt. Sinai (Exodus 32).

When Moses pleaded with God for mercy on behalf of his sister, God granted it, but look at the important lesson He gave her.

> *And Moses cried to the LORD, "O God, please heal her—please." But the LORD said to Moses, "If her father had but spit in her face, should she not be shamed seven days? Let her be shut outside the camp seven days, and after that she may be brought in again." So Miriam was shut outside the camp seven days, and the people did not set out on the march till Miriam was brought in again.* (Numbers 12:13-15)

Only after Miriam had spent time out of the camp did God heal her. Praise God! Miriam became a worshiping warrior for God, and now she was a rightly submitted one. That is God's mercy to take our hearts of rebellion and self-righteousness and turn them into hearts of humbleness and praise. We learn, in this process, to enjoy the juice of the fruit as

He squeezes us and forms our hearts into His own. Resisting this pressure from our loving Father in Heaven can mean we eventually build up resentment toward His teaching and discipline. We can risk becoming hardened and more like the pits of the olive than the oil His heart intends for us to produce. We can end up permanently outside the camp.

> *See to it that no one fails to obtain the grace of God; that no "root of bitterness" springs up and causes trouble, and by it many become defiled.* (Hebrews 12:15)

We do not hear of any other time where Miriam rises up against Moses. She learned something important in God's wilderness. She learned how to obtain the grace of God. This grace that is freely offered to us who believe, allows us to accomplish what we could never accomplish on our own. In Miriam's case, she required God's grace to help her keep her heart submitted the next time she was tempted to sin in her aggravation. God's mercy in healing her gave her the opportunity to learn how to depend on God's grace to stay submitted rightly to the godly authority in her life. God's grace means we don't have to sin or become defiled in order to get our point across. If the point needs to be made, staying rightly submitted means Christ in us can gracefully state our opinion or concern in His perfect love, and we wisely let God do what He decides is best. We trust Him instead of our flesh to accomplish His will in and through us and our spouses and children.

If we have encountered what we perceive as an injustice, God tells us to bring it to Him and leave it there; we are to forgive the offence and ask forgiveness for any offender. Vengeance is mine says the Lord (Romans 12:9). When we take our own perception of God's justice into our own hearts and let it come out of our mouths, I see it as climbing up the lifeguard stand and planting ourselves in authority over the pool when we don't have a license. Nobody wants an unlicensed lifeguard pretending they can keep us safe in a pool. That is what Miriam was doing. God is our lifeguard. He picks who gets to sit in the stand. Sometimes that will be you, and sometimes it won't. We learn to submit to His authority and power and relinquish our own. We will quickly learn that His is better and more effective. It requires of us that we lose our taste for revenge.

> *If possible, as far as it depends on you, live at peace with everyone. Beloved, never avenge yourselves, but leave the way open for [God's] wrath; for it is written, Vengeance is Mine, I will repay (requite), says the Lord. But if your enemy is hungry, feed him; if he is thirsty, give him drink; for by so doing you will heap burning coals upon his head. Do not let yourself be overcome by evil, but overcome (master) evil with good.* (Romans 12:18-21)

Moses had been chosen by God and that meant his anointing (power) was going to flow in authority over Israel. Miriam was not chosen to lead the people, but she was chosen to lead worship and be an encourager. That is where her power would flow. By attacking God's anointed head, she was trying to make her power flow up over his or at least attempt to prove hers matched his. God, in His mercy, showed her how He felt about that in very clear terms. We are all equal before God in Christ, but we each have a job to do in our worship of Him.

I have learned a very important lesson, too. God has placed my authority realms in specific areas for certain times, and I am to learn where and what they are and to stay within them. If I don't learn this important skill, I will be easily pulled off track and distracted by areas or situations that are someone else's responsibility. This is one of Satan's favorite tactics. Our realms of authority will be different depending on what role we are in at the time, and while we hold different roles in the world, in God's eyes it is His authority we are always accountable to. We stand before Him no matter which hat we are wearing.

Pride is really at the root of all rebellion against authority. Pride in our own mindset (what our mind is set on as important or needed, or our "right" perspective) is at the root of most sinful choices to raise our authority up and over those God has chosen to be in control. We make the choice after we have already rationalized in our minds that our choice is right and justified by the injustice or sin we think we see in the other person. It all is really tempting God which is essentially not trusting Him.

> *But each person is tempted when he is lured and enticed by his own desire. Then desire when it has conceived gives birth to sin, and sin when it is fully grown brings forth death.* (James 1:14-15)

As human beings we tend to set our untrained minds against any challenger by using our beliefs, knowledge, experiences and sometimes emotions to try to convince or, in some cases, manipulate, the other person into seeing things our way. God, however, has a different plan for our conflict with perspectives. He uses other people, often our families, to challenge our mindsets in order to reveal our motives and to deepen our faith in Him. He does this in marriage, in family, in our jobs, in our churches, or anywhere He can bring people together to interact over troubling circumstances.

That is what the world is all about. That is why we are in it, to be a light that shines attention onto His mindset which is the only one that should matter. He is fully focused on glorifying Jesus. Until our mindset matches His perfectly, we will struggle. That is His will and it is perfect.

> *I have said these things to you, that in me you may have peace. In the world you will have tribulation. But take heart; I have overcome the world.* (John 16:33)

This scenario in our homes and marriages is not unlike the story of the Sadducees and Pharisees of Jesus' time. Prophets had foretold that there was a Messiah to be expected (Genesis 3:15). They had been told the Messiah would be born of a virgin (Isaiah 7:14), and He would be called the Son of God (Psalm 2:7) and Seed of Abraham (Genesis 22:18). They knew He was to be born in Bethlehem (Micah 5:2), presented with gifts (Psalm 72:10), crucified with thieves (Isaiah 53:12), wounded and smitten (Isaiah 53:5, 50:6), then resurrected (Psalm 16:10) and ascend into heaven (Psalm 68:18). They were told He is coming again (Zechariah 14:4, Ezekiel 39:21-29). That is God's mercy to show them and us these prophecies and there are so many more. Yet, many of the Jews still did not see Jesus as their Messiah, and to this day a veil is laid over their eyes.

> *Since we have such [glorious] hope (such joyful and confident expectation), we speak very freely and openly and fearlessly. Nor [do we act] like Moses, who put a veil over his face so that the Israelites might not gaze upon the finish of the vanishing [splendor which had been upon it]. In fact, their minds were grown hard and calloused [they had become dull and had lost the power of understanding]; for until this present day, when the Old Testament (the old covenant) is being read, that same veil still lies [on their hearts], not being lifted [to reveal] that in Christ it is made void and done away. Yes, down to this [very] day whenever Moses is read, a veil lies upon their minds and hearts. But whenever a person turns [in repentance] to the Lord, the veil is stripped off and taken away.* (2 Corinthians 3:12-16)

Some of us have been in this situation, where the path God suddenly takes us on is so reprehensible to us that we close our eyes and stubbornly refuse to go. We make a decision based on our mindset and are determined to stick to it. We will even look for others that are willing to come into agreement with us so we have a team. We can lean on our fellow conspirators in our stubborn rebellion against God's way. Just like Miriam didn't attack Moses alone, she went into battle with Aaron in agreement. We tend to believe there is safety in numbers. Conspiring for our own way is not going to serve us well; though it may keep us from suffering for a time, it will not stop God's divine will. Avoiding the trials we are supposed to face may leave us with an unprepared heart for what is coming next.

Conspiring for God's desires on the other hand will help us to run His race. Gathering others around us that love Jesus and obey His heart will encourage us to keep going and strengthen us when we feel like giving up. We must be very careful who we allow ourselves to come into agreement with and why.

> *For we are fellow workmen (joint promoters, laborers together) with and for God; you are God's garden and vineyard and field under cultivation, [you are] God's building. According to the grace (the special endowment for my task) of God bestowed on me, like a skillful architect and master builder I laid [the] foundation, and now another [man] is building upon it. But let each [man] be careful how he builds upon it, For no other foundation can anyone lay than that which is [already] laid, which is Jesus Christ (the Messiah, the Anointed One). (1 Corinthians 3:9-11)*

There are many who would see the Pharisees' and Sadducees' stubborn refusal of Jesus and feel justified in giving up on their hearts coming to a sincere faith in Christ. They might forget about them or judge these Pharisees and Sadducees because they had disowned fellow Jewish believers and they disowned Jesus. Have we ever acted like this when we thought we were absolutely right? Be careful, Paul warns, the Israelites in the wilderness were disciplined for much the same heart attitudes. If they were held accountable how much more will we, who have Christ, be accountable for our sins?

> *Nor discontentedly complain as some of them did—and were put out of the way entirely by the destroyer (death). Now these things befell them by way of a figure [as an example and warning to us]; they were written to admonish and fit us for right action by good instruction, we in whose days the ages have reached their climax (their consummation and concluding period). Therefore let anyone who thinks he stands*

> [who feels sure that he has a steadfast mind and is standing firm], take heed lest he fall [into sin]. (1Corinthians 10:10-12)

Based on behaviors like these the world might think they are justified to say to Israel that the Jewish people missed their Savior and that they will never have a relationship with Him and His bride, the Church! Is this accurate? Or are these just some facts that are hiding God's truth? Has the world perhaps missed something crucial in all this judgment between the Church of the New Testament and the Jews of the Old Testament?

There is a sweet story about tradition and truth in *Fiddler on the Roof*, a movie based on a story about Tevye and his daughters.[15] At the end of this story, Tevye—the head of a Jewish family at the turn of twentieth-century Russia—is facing the reality of his heart. He and the entire Russian village where he has lived his whole life are being sent out into the wilderness. These forced evictions of Jewish villages were called pogroms and were hate crimes perpetrated against the Jewish communities in Russia. The Russian government would send an order to evict, and the military was responsible for making the people submit. Soldiers would burn homes and threaten lives as they forced people to leave their homes, stores, and synagogues. There was usually no particular motivation for the pogrom to take place other than power and the desire to show the Jews who had it.

As Tevye is packing up his family and his entire Jewish neighborhood is walking by his door, he is surprised by something unfamiliar. He sees one of his daughters and her husband standing at his gate. They are packed up and are also leaving. He sees that they are going into the wilderness, and he is fully aware that they did not have to. This shakes Tevye's foundations in a way that having to leave his home and facing the unknown does not.

This daughter of his had already challenged everything that was dear to Tevye. She had, against his will and tradition, decided to marry a man

---

[15] Jewison, Norman (Director and Producer). *The Fiddler on the Roof*. Joseph Stein (Screen Play). Based on Tevye and His Daughters by Sholem Aleichem. The Mirisch Production Company. November 3, 1971.

ice. If that wasn't hard enough for him, the man was not   fallen in love with a Russian soldier who taught her about   s. Her choice to embrace the truth of the cross of Christ had gotten her what so many Jews face when they become born again, total rejection. The intense persecution that had been waged against this daughter of Tevye's and her new husband had led them to be completely estranged from the rest of his family for a long time.

What was most unusual about them standing at the gate of Tevye's home was that Russian law would have protected this soldier and his wife from the attacks of the pogrom. They would not have been required or expected to leave their home or village. Her father would have known that fact clearly as he stood gazing at this couple whose love for each other and his people challenged his heart so deeply.

"What is this?!" he demands of the soldier of whom he has convinced himself is the enemy of his family and his people. "What is this?!" The humble and steadfast soldier husband, holding his wife close, says, "I cannot stay when I see how they treat you. I must go."

As we watch, something switches in Tevye's face. His older daughter sees it and takes advantage of the moment, quickly snatching a quick hug. Then they are gone. Tevye turns his face away, but something has changed and we can almost feel it. He must still venture out into the wilderness, but a seed of truth has managed to plant itself in this stubborn man's heart. He will carry this seed with him into the wilderness. Maybe it will take root there and begin to grow.

> *And I will sow her for Myself anew in the land, and I will have love, pity, and mercy for her who had not obtained love, pity, and mercy; and I will say to those who were not My people, You are My people, and they shall say, You are my God!* (Hosea 2:23)

This verse in Hosea was referring to the Gentile, pagan nations that had not been allowed to drink from the sap of the cultivated olive tree.

Mercifully His

In His great mercy God saw fit to reach all the world with the love of Jesus, grafting believing Gentiles into His good tree. Gentiles, the wild olive branches, could now drink of His precious love. In this same mercy, He grafts back into His good tree any of His People Israel who would turn from disbelief to belief.

Will we walk in the full power of His anointing and go wherever He sends us in order to share the news of salvation through Jesus Christ, the long awaited Messiah? The most unmerciful thing we can do to those who still disbelieve is to withhold from them the gospel truth of Christ. They all must hear. Jew, Gentile, male, female, slave or free all have the choice to make. He is the only way, He is the truth, and He is the life.

The word *mercy* in Hosea 2:14 is a Hebrew word *rach*am,[16] which depicts a deep, kindly sympathy or sorrow felt for another who has been struck with affliction or misfortune, accompanied with a desire to relieve the suffering for them. The word occurs forty-seven times in the Old Testament, with God being by far the most common provider and His afflicted people, the most common objects of His *racham*.

The Lord has been compassionate to us. He has forgiven us of our sins and through His Son Jesus Christ we now have access to the Holy of Holies, the most intimate place in His heart. He sent His Son and the disciples to the Jews first and then to the Gentiles (Romans 1:16). When many of the Jewish people would not believe, He permitted the unbelievers to be pruned from the good olive tree so that there would be room for others to be grafted in. He calls their unbelief a temporary blindness. Like the father in *Fiddler on the Roof,* there is a blindness on the part of some of God's people toward those things that others in their family are able to see.

Paul warns us not to become proud and bitter toward God's cut off branches; neither are we to boast toward the olive tree that we have been grafted into, for it is the root that supports us. Jesus is the good tree and

---

[16] The Complete Word Study: Old Testament, King James Version. Zodhiates, Spiros, Th.D.AMG Publishers Chattanooga, TN 37422, USA. 1994. P 2365. #7356 *Racham*.

He is the root. We cling to Him, His mindset must become ours. We are the branches as long as we persist in our belief in Him. There were branches that were on God's tree before Jesus came. They were Israel and all those Gentile individuals who had come to worship the God of Israel, people like Rahab, Ruth, and others.

God's plan from the beginning was to the Jews first and then to the Gentiles. He reassured Elijah concerning this when Elijah pleaded for help from God because he felt as though he was the only Jew left on earth who believed, "Lord, they have killed your prophets, they have demolished your altars, and I alone am left, and they seek my life." (1Kings 19:10). What did God reply to him?

> *And he said, Go forth, and stand upon the mount before the LORD. And, behold, the LORD passed by, and a great and strong wind rent the mountains, and brake in pieces the rocks before the LORD; but the LORD was not in the wind: and after the wind an earthquake; but the LORD was not in the earthquake: And after the earthquake a fire; but the LORD was not in the fire: and after the fire a still small voice…*
> *…I will leave Myself 7,000 in Israel, all the knees that have not bowed to Baal and every mouth that has not kissed him. (1 Kings 19:11-12, 18)*

The still small voice was God and He directed Elijah to return the way he had come to the wilderness of Damascus, and He reassured Elijah that he wasn't alone. He assured him that God's plan was in place to rid the country of Jezebel and Ahab. Most importantly, God told him that He had left for Himself seven thousand in Israel, all whom had not bowed to Baal and whose mouths had not kissed him. There would always be a remnant chosen by grace, not works, so that none can boast.

> *…if God did not spare the natural branches [because of unbelief], neither will He spare you [if you are guilty of the same offense]. Then note and appreciate the gracious kindness and the severity of God:*

severity toward those who have fallen, but God's gracious kindness to you—provided you continue in His grace and abide in His kindness; otherwise you too will be cut off (pruned away). And even those others [the fallen branches, Jews], if they do not persist in [clinging to] their unbelief, will be grafted in, for God has the power to graft them in again. (Romans 11:20-23)

As our Jewish friends and neighbors see God's mercy being given to us, and the fruits of His mercy in us, they may turn and face us as Tevye faced his son-in-law, however briefly. What will you do in that moment when they turn to you? They are curious; they are wondering about you; you stand out to them, and you are different. That is because of Christ's presence in you. They sense Him, they see His love in you and they are drawn toward you. Paul shares God's directive to those of us that are wild olives grafted onto His good tree in Romans:

Many of the people of Israel are now enemies of the Good News, and this benefits you Gentiles. Yet they are still the people He loves because He chose their ancestors Abraham, Isaac, and Jacob. For God's gifts and His call can never be withdrawn. Once, you Gentiles were rebels against God, but when the people of Israel rebelled against Him, God was merciful to you instead. Now they are the rebels, and God's mercy has come to you so that they, too, will share in God's mercy. For God has imprisoned everyone in disobedience so He could have mercy on everyone. (Romans 11:28-32, NLT)

Like the Russian soldier husband in *Fiddler on the Roof* was different because of his heart and the actions that he took from the place of his heart, so must ours be different. His was full of the sincere love of Christ and His mercy, and he spoke and acted from this abundance. We must strive to be like Christ too, full of salt and light. His difference from all the others was why Tevye's daughter had noticed him in the first place. That is why she read his Bible and perhaps found the truth that stirred in her heart was a reflection of her Savior's love for her and her family. The mercy of the Russian soldier husband was hidden from Tevye until it stood out in such stark contrast to the bleak prospects of the wilderness.

Would you have made the same choice that the Russian soldier husband made? He didn't have to go into the wilderness. He had the right and the ability to stay in the home he had built and be safe right where he was. Instead, he chose to act in mercy. It was the harder and more costly choice for his wife and family. What would you have done? What will you do?

If you have accepted Jesus Christ as your Savior and Messiah then you have married into (been grafted into) the vine which is Jesus. These branches (both on and off the tree) are His family and mercy is His mindset. The root of this olive tree is God's covenant to Abraham fulfilled in Jesus Christ our Messiah. The promise to Abraham from God that through his seed, the nations would be blessed (Genesis 22:18).

Seed in Hebrew is a play on words. It is singular, thus pointing to The Seed of Jesus. But, the word *seed* in Hebrew is akin to our word *offspring*, which would also include all the people that would ever come from Abraham through Isaac, the son of promise. Jesus makes it plain to us in His conversation with the Jewish Pharisees and Sadducees that the true children of Abraham are those who are circumcised in the heart, not just the flesh. It is through faith in The Seed, Jesus that we are saved and our hearts circumcised.

We have an assignment from God, a responsibility to His covenant promise made to Abraham. We are to be lights of His mercy and love to the nations, to the Jew first and to the Gentiles. The writer of Hebrews describes it this way:

> *Exercise foresight and be on the watch to look [after one another], to see that no one falls back from and fails to secure God's grace (His unmerited favor and spiritual blessing), in order that no root of resentment (rancor, bitterness, or hatred) shoots forth and causes trouble and bitter torment, and the many become contaminated and defiled by it.* (Hebrews 12:15)

God's anecdote for bitterness is mercy, and if we fail to show mercy to His lost world then we are failing at our assignment. His blood, shed for our sins, speaks of His mercy. When the Russian soldier chose to enter the wilderness with his wife it reflected His understanding of the mercy given to him. Anytime we choose to show mercy we are speaking to our understanding of His blood. When we extend His grace and love by sharing the Good News of Jesus, we are His mercy seat. We may be persecuted, spit at, rejected by family and friends, but we are His mercy in action.

Do you remember back in Chapter Three, I referred to our family as bunches of grapes on the vine and described how our children had learned to travel back and forth from one vineyard to another in our blended family? Eventually our daughter was led to share the gospel with her father's family. This was evidence of the mercy she had received and understood to be real, being shared with those in disbelief so they could come to be grafted into His good tree. There are some believers who might be tempted to look at the disbelieving branches and allow some sense of pride to creep into their hearts. This is not evidence of God's mercy and won't be useful in fulfilling His plan to complete His bride for His return. Our daughter's sharing of the gospel with her father's family brought some persecution in the beginning, but what was important was the stand she took to share the truth.

Jesus did not come to keep peace between people, He came with a gift, the gift of His blood, shed on a cross. He became a curse that we would not be cursed. He died that we would have life and have it abundantly. His blood shed and His resurrection to life is the story of mercy we show and we share.

The world's mercy mindset is wrong and won't ever bring us into right relationship with Jesus. The world hated Him. They hated His offer because their deeds were evil and they preferred them to be kept in the dark (John 3:20). The world of our peers may hate us. I'm pretty sure the majority of the Russian soldier's friends and even family probably didn't understand or agree with his choice.

Mercy generally won't make sense to our own understanding or to others. That is why it disarms them. Satan will resist mercy, because it promises change, a change in a person's walk and perspective that turns them toward the light that is Christ.

Another wilderness shaking is coming (Hebrews 12:18-28). It is ordained to come from God. The choices we make in that shaking will either condemn us or complete us. It is in our completion that the promise to Israel can be kept, the promise to all of us of life from death. What are we to do? We are to be on the watch for each other to show His mercy, to see that no one falls back from His grace so that no roots of bitterness and hatred shoot up and defile others. We are to offer to God pleasing service and acceptable worship, with modesty and pious care and godly fear and awe (Hebrews 12:15, 28). A heart that has learned to trust in Jesus alone for our all is the vessel that will carry His mercy to the world.

> *But now I am speaking to you who are Gentiles. Inasmuch then as I am an apostle to the Gentiles, I lay great stress on my ministry and magnify my office, In the hope of making my fellow Jews jealous [in order to stir them up to imitate, copy, and appropriate], and thus managing to save some of them. For if their rejection and exclusion from the benefits of salvation were [overruled] for the reconciliation of a world to God, what will their acceptance and admission mean? [It will be nothing short of] life from the dead!* (Rom 11:13-15)

Chapter 8

COMPLETELY HIS

Yes, furthermore, I count everything as loss compared to the possession of the priceless privilege (the overwhelming preciousness, the surpassing worth, and supreme advantage) of knowing Christ Jesus my Lord and of progressively becoming more deeply and intimately acquainted with Him [of perceiving and recognizing and understanding Him more fully and clearly]. For His sake I have lost everything and consider it all to be mere rubbish (refuse, dregs), in order that I may win (gain) Christ (the Anointed One). (Philippians 3:8)

> Motel: [on being evicted] "Rabbi, we've been waiting all our lives for the Messiah. Wouldn't now be a good time for Him to come?"
> Rabbi: "We'll have to wait for Him somewhere else. Meanwhile, let's start packing."[17]

DO WE ALL have a drug of choice? Something we turn to in order to escape what we don't like doing or feeling or facing? It can be alcohol, drugs, the newspaper, jobs, knowledge, family or any other host of things. Whatever it is, if we keep turning to it in hard

---

17 Jewison, Norman (Director and Producer). *The Fiddler on the Roof*. Joseph Stein (Screen Play). Based on Tevye and His Daughters by Sholem Aleichem. The Mirisch Production Company. November 3, 1971.

situations instead of Christ, it will disconnect us from hearing or knowing Jesus. Ultimately, this "drug" has to fail us so we have the opportunity to turn to the true source of our security and love, Jesus. My marriage and my new family had become my drug of choice and I refused to see that there was something terribly wrong with both. Before marriage, the drug had been my job and my child. Marriage changes things. Something happens when two become one and everything in them becomes double portioned. That means that all the good stuff in my husband and I doubled (awesome) and all the bad stuff doubled too. When bad stuff doubles in size and power, it gets easier to see it. The same thing happens when we ask Jesus to take over our lives and hearts. This "marriage" to Jesus allows His pure light to shine in even the darkest corners of our hearts and souls. His light reveals the good and the bad.

It took asking Jesus into my heart to shed light on what my family really needed. They did not need me to worship them, they needed me to love them and discipline is love (Hebrews 12:5-11). If we are going to help our families and churches stay connected to Christ, we must discipline in love. I believe that the Church has begun to move in a direction that could lead her away from the light offered by her bridegroom, Jesus. As I watch leaders begin the dangerous path of rejecting His commandments about marriage and purity, I fear for their intimacy with their Lord and Savior. It is in losing track, or never knowing who Jesus truly is and what He has for us, that the Church could begin to pretend to still be married even while they are actually living in separate rooms from Him and leading different lives than what He has called them to live.

> *I am the Lord God. I created the heavens like an open tent above. I made the earth and everything that grows on it. I am the source of life for all who live on this earth, so listen to what I say... I am the LORD; that is my name! I will not give my glory to another or my praise to idols.* (Isaiah 42:5, 8)

Listening to and agreeing with Him, however, will not glorify Him unless we also submit to Him and obey the commands contained in His Word. From everlasting to everlasting the LORD's love is with those who fear him, and His righteousness is with their children's children—with those who keep his covenant and remember to obey his precepts (Psalm 103:17-18). Jesus reiterated the idea that glorifying and loving God are one and the same when He told us in John 14:15: "If you love me, you will obey what I command."

John's, my, and our family's calling is to share a key principle that drew us closer to Jesus and directed our feet to the path that follows His light and bids us to wait and obey His direction. This key opened a door to a bridge between our Jewish neighbors and our family even as it drew us deeper into Christ.

> *For we are God's [own] handiwork (His workmanship), recreated in Christ Jesus, [born anew] that we may do those good works which God predestined (planned beforehand) for us [taking paths which He prepared ahead of time], that we should walk in them [living the good life which He prearranged and made ready for us to live].* (Ephesians 2:10)

Jew and Gentile were always meant to become one new man in Christ Jesus our Messiah (Ephesians 2:15). I liken this to marriage, which was designed by God to create one flesh from two individuals and this is a mystery. Becoming 'one' requires a great struggle as our flesh is made to submit to the holy law of love that asks us to do what doesn't make sense to our emotions and sensibilities. This struggle sometimes calls us to break apart, or stand separate to show our unique colors in the form of unique talents and giftings, while at other times it requires us to blend together in unity and submission to one another in Christ. The closer we draw toward Him in these struggles for unity, the more we reflect His light to the dark world.

I believe that when we tire of the struggle, we let down our arms and begin to lose the fight for the truth. Without the truth, our faith means nothing and compromise with the world will steal the power of Christ from our hearts and homes. When I stopped struggling for what I believed to be true about Jesus in my family, we began to fall apart, and I began to lose faith. When the Church decided to separate from her Jewish brothers and sisters by taking issue with the celebrating of feasts and days, the Church inadvertently participated in a divorce which left us without each other's special gifts and talents. Without each other the struggle loosened and the sharpening ceased. Many essential truths of Christ's character were lost to both groups. Becoming fully mature in the mind of Christ requires a love for other believers that is only grown in the heat of godly conflict, struggle and sharpening. Godly conflict produces a heat that sanctifies and purifies and allows for the process of becoming one. Unity empowers us through the required struggle of remaining one even as we each grow and change. I believe the time has come to see the one new man manifested in the power that is meant to draw the cut off branches to be grafted back into their own cultivated olive tree. The training for this struggle will begin in our homes, in our marriages, in our neighborhoods, and, ultimately, in the Church as a whole.

> *Compromise with the world will steal the power of Christ from our hearts and homes.*

> *For if you were cut from what is by nature a wild olive tree, and grafted, contrary to nature, into a cultivated olive tree, how much more will these, the natural branches, be grafted back into their own olive tree. (Romans 11:24)*

The path our family was led to was one that followed the Biblical calendar and God's directives for His year. We followed this path with the

Completely His

help of dear friends who had walked out this truth before us. While we had expected to get to know Jesus more deeply, we found that in the process, we also fell in love with His people, Israel. We believe that a dedicated church of believers who are earnestly praying for His people and for their peace in Christ will be participating as His instruments in bringing the pruned branches back into the intimacy of their own olive tree. Like the prodigal son's return, God looks for His peoples' full return. If we are purely His, so should we be looking for God's people to return to their land and for their realization of Jesus, Y'shua, as their Messiah.

There is a caution, however, in revving-up the engine of the Biblical feasts that needs to be addressed. Like giving the keys of the family car to our teenagers the first time, a wise parent shares the sage advice gained from experience. Celebrating the feasts to please man or to be included in a group of people is not the reason to celebrate. Nonetheless, keeping these appointed times with our Savior in order to get to know Him on a purer level is. Observing the biblical feasts can lead us into a deeper and more compassionate understanding of our Jewish brothers and sisters, but it can also put us back under bondage to the law. It can steal our salvation hope in Christ alone and diminish His work accomplished for our sins on the cross. It has the potential to do exactly what has happened in the Universalist churches and in any other church that has put the doctrines of man in competition with the Word made flesh, who is Jesus.

Following the feasts as the Jewish people do, and did, was fascinating and taught us much. We began to question, however, why we would celebrate these feasts or special days in the same way as traditional Jewish people. If the majority of Jewish people are as far away from biblical Judaism as many Christians are from biblical Christianity, then our feasting should also look different from theirs. Not necessarily as different as Santa Claus and the Easter bunny, but it should look and be different because we are supposed to be worshipping in the Spirit of God with Messiah Jesus as the focus. While Santa Claus and the Easter bunny are cute for children's fun and sweet teeth, they do not teach us the truth about Jesus. We will not be judged based on a score card of how many nice things we have done versus how many naughty things. His judgement will be righteous and will be focused on how we learned to love with His love. (Matthew 25:31-46, Matthew 7:11).He finds no pleasure in following traditions of men at the cost of the purity of Christ.

> *But He said to them, Excellently and truly [so that there will be no room for blame] did Isaiah prophesy of you, the pretenders and hypocrites, as it stands written: These people [constantly] honor Me with their lips, but their hearts hold off and are far distant from Me. In vain (fruitlessly and without profit) do they worship Me, ordering and teaching [to be obeyed] as doctrines the commandments and precepts of men. (Mark 7:6-7)*

Jews today have embraced a Judaism that was constructed to adapt to life without the temple sacrifices. This is called Rabbinical Judaism and it doesn't recognize that the new temple was rebuilt in the hearts of the believer who has been made new in Christ. If a Jewish person doesn't yet recognize Jesus as their Messiah, their feasting isn't supposed to be fulfilling. It is instead a snare and a trap (Romans 11:9). For them, these ritual observances are still a rehearsal for the day when God reveals Himself to them as Jesus, their Messiah. I believe He will do this and that it is our call and command to go to the Jew first and tell them about Jesus from a heart full of His love that looks for the pruned, cultivated branches to be restored to their own, good tree (Romans 11). It will mean life from death for the Church, composed of Jew and Gentile, when this plan is followed and we are made complete.

> *And David says, "Let their table become a snare and a trap, a stumbling block and a retribution for them;... So I ask, did they stumble in order that they might fall? By no means! Rather through their trespass*

> *salvation has come to the Gentiles, so as to make Israel jealous. Now if their trespass means riches for the world, and if their failure means riches for the Gentiles, how much more will their full inclusion mean! Now I am speaking to you Gentiles…., I magnify my ministry in order somehow to make my fellow Jews jealous, and thus save some of them. For if their rejection means the reconciliation of the world, what will their acceptance mean but life from the dead?* (Romans 11:9-15)

We who have embraced Him as our bridegroom, we who have come to know who He really is, are to be built up as a temple to Him, and we hunger for more than a shadow of Him. We reach forward for the real thing, the Spirit of God who has come to dwell in us and make His holy home in our hearts. He is the living God in us. It is to this new temple, full of His presence and purity of love that the Jews are to be drawn, impressed by and jealous for what they see living in and through us. What we require as believers in Christ and should actively pursue, is more and more truth and pure expression of Him. We celebrate the feasts, not with the old leaven but instead with the new leaven of sincerity and truth in the love of Christ (1 Corinthians 5:7-8). When we have taken hold of His Spirit, we believe that His feasts become a rehearsal for our impending marriage to Him. If we celebrate them from sheer knowledge or command without a heart full of His changing love, we risk becoming the Pharisees of our day.

> *For I would not, brethren, that ye should be ignorant of this mystery, lest ye should be wise in your own conceits; that blindness in part is happened to Israel, until the fullness of the Gentiles be come in. And so all Israel shall be saved: as it is written, There shall come out of Sion the Deliverer, and shall turn away ungodliness from Jacob: For this is my covenant unto them, when I shall take away their sins.* (Romans 11:25-27)

The word 'fullness' comes from a Greek word *pleroma*[18] meaning 'completeness and reaching the intended goal of being filled up'. According to Ephesians 4:13, the goal is to the attainment of the state and stature of Christ, to full maturity in Christian knowledge and love. In a word, it means wholeness. It means whole dependence on Him for everything and every direction. If walking out the seven feasts[19] of the Lord draws us into a more intimate relationship with His Spirit whose purpose is to teach us to glorify Him, then our fullness may be achieved to some degree by rehearsing them. If the feasts practiced in the fullness of His Spirit will encourage the re-grafting of His people, Israel, into the good tree of Jesus, which means life from death for the world, then why aren't we seeking this with our whole heart?

> *For if their rejection means the reconciliation of the world, what will their acceptance mean but life from the dead?* (Romans 11:15)

One very important thing must happen, we must be growing in our hearts the seed of Abraham. That seed, or offspring which led us to receive Christ (Galatians 3), is to fill us so completely that we grow into a fruitful branch bearing good fruit for His Kingdom. As we are pruned our fruit will become so bountiful that the breath of God may blow the seed of our fruit to the Jews and Gentiles. Our prayer is that they will receive that seed in the soil of their hearts and grow fruit that is to the glory of Jesus, their Messiah. THEN the bride will be unified. In the power of that unity the river of the Holy Spirit will flow out to the nations and a tree will grow along its banks that will bear fruit for the health of the nations (Ezekiel 47). We keep these feasts to know Him

---

18 The Complete Word Study: New Testament, King James Version. Zodhiates, Spiros, Th.D. AMG Publishers Chattanooga, TN 37422, USA. 1991. P. 948. *Pleroma*.

19 The Lord commanded all His people, in the First Covenant (Tanach, esp Leviticus 23), to celebrate eight special "Appointed Times" (Moadim). They are also called Holy Convocations or Feasts (Midraei Kodesh). They are: 1. Sabbath (Shabbat); 2. Passover (Pesach); 3. Unleavened Bread (Matzah); 4.Firstfruits to Weeks/Pentecost (Bikkurim—Shavuot); 5. Trumpets (Yom Tru'a); 6. Day of Atonement (Yom Kippur); and 7. Booths or Tabernacles (Succot).

more and to plant the pure seed of Abraham in the hearts of nations where it will grow in good soil, fertilized by the pure love of a matured and unified Church that seeks His will, not their own.

To the Jew First and then the Gentile

A few years ago, I saw the fruit of celebrating the feasts in the fulfillment of Jesus. Our neighbors are Jewish and, unknown to me, they were noticing our family growing in the Lord and practicing the biblical feasts. I don't know if it was because we were going to worship on Saturdays, or for other reasons, but one day, the father of this family came across the street to me and shared a list he had compiled in preparation for Yom Kippur. Yom Kippur is not a pilgrimage feast, but it is important to know that it is the day that Jews believe their names are sealed in the Book of Life, or not. His list was related to this day, and we were able to have a wonderful conversation about our God. Soon after that, God prompted me to share my testimony of Jesus and how I came to know He is the Messiah who came for the Jews and through them, offered salvation to the world.

Jesus is the way, the truth, and the life. Everything we do must be for His glory and purpose, or it will be for our own glory and purpose. Our purposes, apart from Christ, can do nothing. At first, I hesitated when God prompted me to share the Gospel with our Jewish neighbors. I knew it might cost me a valued friendship. If I had continued to hesitate I might have missed the exact time God had prepared for their hearts to receive.

His glory is to have His people Israel restored and made whole through Him. He has provided the way, Jesus, and we, Jew and Gentile together in Christ, are His bride. Do we love Him enough to pay the cost of building up His kingdom here on earth, and are we willing to relinquish our own? His Kingdom is the kingdom that has been designed and intended from the beginning to hold all who would believe.

> *The thief comes only in order to steal and kill and destroy. I came that they may have and enjoy life, and have it in abundance (to the full, till it overflows).* (John 10:10)

The Book of Acts tells readers that the first apostles continued to celebrate the biblical feasts and to follow the Hebrew calendar. Wherever possible, they continued to obey God's command to gather together in Jerusalem for the pilgrimage feasts. The law that said they had to attend these feasts or be found unrighteous had been fulfilled in Christ (Matthew 5:17-20). Their desire to participate came now from a love for Jesus and His perfect plan, not a fear of retribution. They believed Jesus when He told them to the Jew first and then the Gentile. Paul himself made a habit of first entering the synagogue in every city he encountered, preaching to the Jews until God indicated otherwise, releasing him then to go on to the Gentiles or to the next city (Acts 15; Romans 1:16).

When did this pattern change? Why did it change? How did we go from worshipping Jesus as the fulfilled promise of the Torah and prophets to celebrating Jesus in a whole new set of doctrines based largely on pagan worship of works, intellect, and prosperity? One answer could be that the struggle to turn an ever-increasing number of Gentiles to an unfamiliar calendar proved to be too daunting for the early Church.

The Jewish calendar by which the Jewish feasts are given their dates is very different from the western calendar. The Hebrew calendar is not a straightforward lunar calendar, but every time there is a new moon, that indicates a new Jewish month called Rosh Hodesh, which means head of the month. Passover is always on the fourteenth day of the month Nissan according to God's command in the Torah, which is to be the first month of the year (Exodus 12:2). The western calendar does not follow the moon's movements, so the cycle of the Jewish year is different. Setting the calendar dates according to the moon or lunar cycles also coincided with agricultural practices of soil preparation, seed planting, first fruit observances, and harvesting. Using a lunar calendar, however, the process to create and fix dates was not a simple one. Sometimes Jewish holidays were celebrated twice when there was a discrepancy about the precise day, or during times when the Israelites weren't permitted in their Temple. A particular holiday might be celebrated later in the calendar year or be declared to be a new holiday, as was the case with a perhaps delayed Sukkot celebration coming to be called Chanukah.

During the diaspora[20], when many Jews still lived outside the walls of Jerusalem, these dates had to be communicated over long distances, which was often accomplished by messengers or beacons. Sometimes messages might be delayed or beacons misunderstood or changed, and dates and information could become confused. This is one reason why Paul reassures us in Romans that we are not to worry if we get the exact dates right for our celebrations. It is the motives and focus of our hearts that Jesus is jealous over.

> *One man esteems one day as better than another, while another man esteems all days alike [sacred]. Let everyone be fully convinced (satisfied) in his own mind. He who observes the day, observes it in honor of the Lord. He also who eats, eats in honor of the Lord, since he gives thanks to God; while he who abstains, abstains in honor of the Lord and gives thanks to God. None of us lives to himself [but to the Lord], and none of us dies to himself [but to the Lord, for].* (Romans 14:5-7)

As believers, according to the Book of Acts, The Way[21] began to include more and more Gentile believers. In the years after the destruction of the temple in Jerusalem, the friction between them and their unbelieving Jewish family and friends increased. Until the martyrdom

---

20 The term diaspora in ancient Greek means "a scattering or sowing of seeds" and refers to any people or ethnic population forced or induced to leave its traditional homeland. It is here used in reference to the Jewish Diaspora which began in 8th and 6th Centuries BC when Israel was forced into exile from the northern kingdom to Assyria and then from the southern kingdom of Judah to Babylon. The Jews continued to live largely as a diasporan people until the establishment of the state of Israel in 1948.
21 The Way: A term commonly understood to describe believers in the early church. Acts 9:2

of Stephen, which is described in Acts 7, the believers and non-believers co-existed and worshipped in the synagogues. This is why the Jerusalem Council found it unimportant that the Gentile believers be required to know the law in order to be considered true believers as it was taught in the synagogues every Sabbath (Acts 15:21). The council's point to the Gentile believers and their believing Jewish brothers and sisters was this: There is no need that new Gentile believers convert, be physically circumcised, or have to learn all the laws before they begin their walk in Christ. Requiring these things from them would put a burden on them too heavy to bear, a burden that Christ said He died for so we would not be required to carry. His burden is light. Therefore, the council warned, be wary of those that would impose laws on believers. Following even one law with a heart that thinks it must in order for salvation jeopardizes the walk of faith that assures us He has fulfilled the law; that walk which trusts solely in Christ's work on the cross and His ever growing work in our hearts to complete this fulfillment of the law of love in our souls.

After the martyrdom of Stephen, many believers in The Way left Jerusalem because of great persecution and centered themselves at Antioch. This was where the believers in The Way were first called Christians (Acts 11:26). Persecution continued to spread believers all over the Middle East and eventually into Rome, Italy. What the devil had intended for evil, God used to disperse His gospel to the nations.

In AD 60, most Roman leaders still saw Christianity and Judaism as the same religion. Judaism in first-century Rome enjoyed a legally protected status under Roman rule, but Christianity did not, and this became a dividing rod between them. When Rome burned during Emperor Nero's reign, possibly by his own hand, he looked for a scapegoat and found one in the minority group of Christians. Many Christians during this time were searched out, imprisoned, and burned at the stake. At the same time in Jerusalem, Herod discovered favor within the unbelieving Jewish community for imprisoning and killing Jewish believers in Messiah. Within seven years, Peter, Paul, and James had been killed for their faith and the Christian church became largely centered outside of Jerusalem.

By AD 70, the second temple in Jerusalem was destroyed and there followed a Jewish/Roman war called, The Great Revolt. Jewish and Gentile believers in Jerusalem, many of whom still attended the synagogues there, did not want to fight by the sword against the Romans, and the Jewish unbelievers saw this as treason against their people. As intense persecution against all the Jews grew and Rome fought to take back control, more and more believers fled or were forced to leave. The Romans determined for this to be a final cleansing of Jerusalem and even went so far as to rename the region Syria-Palaestina hoping to discourage the Jews from ever coming back.

Christianity later found favor in an Emperor named Constantine who eventually professed his belief in the Christian faith. This helped usher in a period of favor and relative peace for believers in the land but also began the growth of a new approach to faith in Christ. This new direction rejected the doctrines of Biblical feasts and days. Through a series of council decisions, Roman Christianity became characterized as one that embraced pagan dates that had once celebrated other gods and goddesses. Constantine himself kept his pagan symbols on his coins and armor as he added his vision of the cross alongside the picture of the goddess of the sun. This Roman Christianity took the worship times familiar and traditional to the Roman Empire and now included the gospel story of Jesus. Eventually the Roman faith set up a new leadership model including Popes, Cardinals and Bishops and outlawed the biblical practices that recognized the feast days and celebrations.

In AD 325, relations between the Rabbinic Jewish community and the Roman Christians had deteriorated significantly. There was hostility in both directions and Church leaders decided at the Council of Nicaea, to take matters into their own hands:

> It was declared to be particularly unworthy for this, the holiest of all festivals, to follow the custom of the Jews, who had soiled their hands with the most fearful of crimes, and whose minds were blinded. In rejecting their custom, we may transmit to our descendants the legitimate mode of celebrating Easter....we ought not, therefore, to have anything in common with the Jews, for the Savior has shown us another way....we desire, dearest brethren, to separate ourselves from the detestable company of the Jews..." (From "Letter of the Emperor to all those not present at the Council: Eusebius, Vita Const., Lib iii, 18-20)

Essentially a divorce decree was agreed upon. Through this decree and others— including the Council of Laodicea in AD 363, which outlawed the Saturday Sabbath in favor of Sunday—the Church freed itself from a marriage that had proven difficult and challenging. The Church effectively refused to enter the wilderness of conflict where they would have had the opportunity to search out a unity pleasing to God. They didn't love the Jewish people enough to stay committed in the struggle. They refused to see their essential wholeness was snugly wrapped in an effort to see this marriage through all the way to Jesus coming again. They saw giants in the land that could hurt them and so they gave up the feasts and their teaching of redemption and restoration and forced that decision on others. They turned instead to their pagan traditions and the teachings which were more familiar to them, mixing into these practices the gospel of Jesus Christ. These newly created days were, in turn, totally alien to the Jewish believers and became more and more alien to the Jews. They would never be made jealous over a faith that now appeared to have absolutely nothing to do with the God of Abraham, Isaac, and Jacob and a lot more to do with the goddess Esther (Easter) and Saint Nicolas.

Over the centuries that would follow, both groups were becoming lost to the truth as each refused to struggle with each other to create something truly new in Christ that would reflect the unity that Jesus had prayed would be true of His bride. It is in godly struggle and conflict that healing and restoration can happen. Avoiding it turns our heads from His hope and leads us down dangerous paths of self-made religious doctrines and act after act of self-preservation, and can ultimately end in the loss of the truth, which is Jesus. It spoils our souls and our roots begin to rot away which leads to a spoiled tree, which will prove unable to stand the winds of persecution and change.

Satan wants the Jews separated from Christ forever as he himself is separated. With this goal of hate in mind, Satan has tried to annihilate the Jewish people during Esther's time by the heart of Haman, and during our time through Hitler. As long as we allow Satan to whisper his lies into our ears against God's people, convincing some that God is no longer watching and expecting their return to His heart, we participate in the delay of the restoration of Israel to their Messiah. When we listen and don't actively dispute Satan on this point, we allow him some say in the healing and completing of the church, and we relinquish to him some of the power entrusted to us to keep the world focused on the hope that is in Christ. Satan wants us to believe that we have not been given the power and love to reach completion in Christ. He is a liar and wants us to stay in pits of fear, hopelessness, and self-righteous anger toward the Jewish people whom God longs for in honor of their forefathers. Jesus wants His bride complete and totally under His banner and built on His rock. Greater is the Spirit in us, then the spirit in the world.

> *From the point of view of the Gospel (good news), they [the Jews, at present] are enemies [of God], which is for your advantage and benefit. But from the point of view of God's choice (of election, of divine selection), they are still the beloved (dear to Him) for the sake of their forefathers. For God's gifts and His call are irrevocable.* (Romans 11:28-29)

To complete His purpose for coming into the world (that we would be one as He and the Father are one), and to be with Him where He is. We must continue to pray, preach, reach, and desire our Jewish unbelieving neighbors to come to the knowledge of their Savior, Jesus Christ

Even as the prodigal son's father kept watching and expecting, that is how we must stand. Our hearts are being tested and refined in the waiting and persevering. When the prodigal son returned to the father and repented, his father was ready with a merciful heart and open arms. It was the older, law abiding brother, that found issue. The older brother's heart had grown proud and boastful in his self-righteousness. The older brother didn't choose to be dressed properly for the feast and didn't join the father in the celebration.

> *But if some of the branches were broken off, while you, a wild olive shoot, were grafted in among them to share the richness [of the root and sap] of the olive tree, do not boast over the branches and pride yourself at their expense. If you do boast and feel superior, remember it is not you that support the root, but the root [that supports] you.* (Romans 11:17-18)

We need to remember that we are grafted into His olive tree only by faith. This gift of faith gives us eyes to see. This gift is from Jesus Himself, not because of anything we have done or earned, only by His grace. This is true so we can't boast in anything but Him. Any boasting in ourselves is pride, and Jesus will resist the proud. True faith also requires us to take action. We are called to obey in faith and to do what God has called us to do or we risk our secure attachment to His good olive tree. Without a faith that acts, James warns us we may be without faith and thus we could be pruned off just as the unbelieving Jews were when they failed to believe. Ignorance or apathy for God's will for the Church, including Israel, breeds arrogance. A conceited Church is a

Church resistant to God, for God opposes the proud but gives grace to the humble (James 4:6).

In the last century, there have been huge changes in the hearts of His people as the Spirit has been more and more embraced by believers, and worshiping in Spirit and truth has led some to seek Him more. A struggle has been allowed in the hearts of His Church, and they are beginning to heal and restore the bridge between Jew and Gentile that was destroyed all those centuries ago. More and more Jews have come to know the Lord, Yeshua, Jesus our Messiah in the last nineteen years especially. This group of Jewish believers is meant to bring refreshing to the Church and in this new re-marriage, we will see the hope for the completeness and wholeness of God's church.

> *So repent (change your mind and purpose); turn around and return [to God], that your sins may be erased (blotted out, wiped clean), that times of refreshing (of recovering from the effects of heat, of reviving with fresh air) may come from the presence of the Lord.* (Acts 3:19-21)

THE CHURCH IN THE WILDERNESS

When we ask Jesus to pass—over the threshold of our hearts and become our Lord and Savior, we are opening the door of our hearts to His life. If we also invite Him in to eat with us, we are opening our hearts to His truth. When we allow Him to become a permanent part of our house and are born again in Him, our hearts are permanently changed. It is at that moment that God seals us with His Holy Spirit and He sees us as complete, perfected, and totally separated from our sinful natures that once held us prisoner.

This position in God is fact but it takes a committed walk with our Savior to truly make Him Lord of all. He sees the end result from the beginning, and that should give us great hope and encouragement. No matter how many times we mess up, if we are willing to acknowledge the sin and not pretend, and we cry out and turn to Him, He promises He will answer. His Spirit will increasingly take control of our heart and He will genuinely change us. Our trust of Christ in us will see us through the darkest of times because He will be the only Spirit directing our steps. In Him we are already full and overflowing because He is full and overflowing. As we lose our lives and empty our souls to His Spirit, we learn that in Him we must make our journey of faith take action. Our true fullness is tested and realized when, in faith, we act on what we say we believe, especially in the heat of persecution.

Persecution is the tool that God has allowed for the strengthening and deepening of our faith. Without this testing we would be in danger of becoming useless, weak, and easily swayed by false doctrines and man's traditions. We are to rejoice when the fiery trials of persecution come because they are allowed in order to reveal in us what is not His, then train us up to be fierce competitors for the crown of life.

> *Blessed are you when they revile and persecute you and say all kinds of evil against you falsely for My sake. Rejoice and be exceedingly glad, for great is your reward in heaven, for so they persecuted the prophets who were before you. You are the salt of the earth; but if the salt loses its flavor, how shall it be seasoned? It is then good for nothing but to be thrown out and trampled underfoot by men.* (Matthew 5:11-13, NKJ)

Jesus called His people to be the salt of the earth. Salt (a Christian) is a preservative that slows decay. It is the character of our faith, tested by trial and affliction that produces 'saltiness' in us that will encourage others and us to keep going and stay in the race. The opposite of this would be a compromised Christian, one whose fear has kept them from risking true intimacy in Christ. They will allow their hearts to become lukewarm because they have mixed the world's coldness toward Christ and His Word into the fire that their soul once had for Him. Lukewarm

Completely His

Christians in an increasingly antagonistic world are on a dangerous slope to becoming cold hearted. We cannot serve two masters. Salt that has lost its savour (saltiness) is good for nothing. A heart grown icy cold cannot fruit His harvest of love.

The Greek word for *lost its saltiness* is *mōranthēi* and is a verb that comes from the word *mōros* which means dull, sluggish, stupid, foolish and to play the fool, to become foolish.[22] It was a common sight in the Middle East during Bible times to see salt scattered in piles on the ground because it had lost its flavor. It had become the most worthless thing imaginable.

> *Salt is good (beneficial), but if salt has lost its saltiness, how will you restore [the saltiness to] it? Have salt within yourselves, and be at peace and live in harmony with one another.* (Mark 9:50)

Salt is a clear, brittle mineral used to flavor, preserve and deice. It is obtained through mining and evaporation, and it must be crushed and ground before it can be useful. Like salt, Christian faith must be pressed, crushed, and tested before it can be empowered completely by His Spirit and used by God to help others. Interestingly, the verse above from Mark 9:50 is taken from the directive in Leviticus 2:13.

> *Every cereal offering you shall season with salt [symbol of preservation]; neither shall you allow the salt of the covenant of your God to be lacking from your cereal offering; with all your offerings you shall offer salt.* (Leviticus 2:13)

The Hebrew word for *salt* is *melach* and actually means powder, or to be easily pulverized or dissolved.[23] When we vow to keep our saltiness,

---

22 The Complete Word Study: New Testament. King James Version. Zodhiates, Spiros, Th.D. AMG Publishers Chattanooga, TN 37422, USA. 1991. The Greek Dictionary of the New Testament. P.49. #3474 *Moros*.
23 The Complete Word Study: Old Testament. King James Version. Zodhiates, Siros, Th. D. AMG Publishers Chattanooga, TN 37422, USA. 1994. The Hebrew and Chaldee Dictionary. P.67. #4417 *Melach*.

we become useful for His purpose of unifying His people. We can be used to sprinkle salt on others, thus preserving their faith in times of persecution and trial. We decide to allow Him in us to break our old, worldly vessel and form us into His vessels of healing and preservation. The Greek word for salt in Matthew 5:13 and Mark 9:50 is *halas*, which means *prudence*.[24] Prudence is defined in Webster's 1828 dictionary in the following manner:

> *Prudence is wisdom applied to practice. It implies caution in deliberating and consulting on the most suitable means to accomplish valuable purposes, and the exercise of sagacity in discerning and selecting them. Prudence differs from wisdom in this, that prudence implies more caution and reserve than wisdom, or is exercised more in foreseeing and avoiding evil, than in devising and executing that which is good. It is sometimes mere caution or circumspection. Prudence is principally in reference to actions to be done, and due means, order, season and method of doing or not doing.*[25]

I can speak for our family in saying that the calamities that hit us during our wilderness journey pulverized our own worldly foundations. We watched as God fractured our outer walls that were made up of our idols. He broke off security that came from self-trust, wealth, intelligence, education (this was big), and talents. The persecution we encountered created a lot of conflict and it was good for us. We learned to keep turning to Him and His Word. This allowed His Spirit to breach our fallen walls of self so He could make us salty for Him.

Turning toward Him in each situation that presses and afflicts us, we are essentially inviting Him to deal with our worldly values and priorities. His love for us dissolves our icy hearts and we begin to soften toward

---

[24] The Complete Word Study: New Testament. King James Version. Zodhiates, Spiros, Th.D. AMG Publishers Chatanooga, TN 37422, USA. 1991. The Greek Dictionary of the New Testament. P.9. #217 *Halas*.

[25] Webster, Noah. American Dictionary of the English Language. 1967 reprint of 1828 edition. Foundation for American Christian Education. *Prudence*.

each other. Over time the conflicts and differences that once threatened to divide us become the glue that unifies. This is perhaps what Peter is referring to when he says that by our obedience to the truth through the Holy Spirit we have purified our hearts for the sincere affection of the brethren. Peter tells us to see that we love one another fervently from a pure heart (1 Peter 1:22). When we agree to lose our own stubborn securities we are agreeing to stop fighting our battles with our own heart, soul, strength, and minds. Our ways will only succeed in getting more of our own ways, which will keep us prisoner from His way. It is only on His path, following His way that we will truly find life and love.

> *And the love of the great body of people will grow cold because of the multiplied lawlessness and iniquity.* (Matthew 24:12)

As the persecutions and trials against the Church begin to intensify and the apostasies and false prophets from within the church increase, the love of most toward Christ and His doctrine—as well as the love they have toward one another—will grow cold. Some will openly desert the faith, corrupt the faith, or grow indifferent about the faith. These will be those believers who would not break, whose knowledge of doctrine and love for the law have refused to allow their walls of self-defense to crumble. This will also include those who rejected the law and chose only to believe in Grace, never submitting their rebellious hearts to His loving discipline. His Spirit has not been allowed to infiltrate their deceived hearts and so they now teach others from a pool that is not pure in His love.

Our ways will only succeed in getting more of our own ways

> *Then they will hand you over to suffer affliction and tribulation and put you to death, and you will be hated by all nations for My name's sake. And then many will be offended and repelled and will begin*

> *to distrust and desert [Him Whom they ought to trust and obey] and will stumble and fall away and betray one another and pursue one another with hatred. And many false prophets will rise up and deceive and lead many into error. And the love of the great body of people will grow cold because of the multiplied lawlessness and iniquity.* (Matthew 24:9-12)

Those believers with extra oil, who have been to the wilderness and come out humbled by His love and full of the power of the Holy Spirit, will be salt and light to a darkening world. They will defend the faith and preach the truth of the Gospel of Christ. They will be His faithful servants telling the truth of the Jesus and feeding their households with the bread and water of life.

> *But he who endures to the end will be saved. And this good news of the kingdom (the Gospel) will be preached throughout the whole world as a testimony to all the nations, and then will come the end.* (Matthew 24:13-14)

Jesus tells us in the Book of Matthew to understand that had we known in what part of the night the thief was coming (to attack us with his lawlessness), we would have watched and not allowed our houses to be undermined and broken into. Because we don't know the exact times and days all will occur, we are to be continually ready. Jesus is coming at an hour we do not expect Him. If we have allowed hardness of heart, hate, bitterness, and rancor to rob our homes of His love, then we risk Jesus finding us in a state of heart that demands His judgment instead of His promised intimacy.

We are to be feeding our families and friends with the truth of Christ, supplying them with the necessary tools to run the race of faith, and all in His timing and care. We are to be nurturing His bride to prepare to become His love under the *huppa* of His wedding feast (Matthew 24:43-51).

> *Blessed (happy, fortunate, and to be envied) is that servant whom, when his master comes, he will find so doing (giving food and supplies at the proper time) I solemnly declare to you, he will set him over all his possessions. But if that servant is wicked and says to himself, My master is delayed and is going to be gone a long time, And begins to beat his fellow servants and to eat and drink with the drunken, The master of that servant will come on a day when he does not expect him and at an hour of which he is not aware, And will punish him [cut him up by scourging] and put him with the pretenders (hypocrites); there will be weeping and grinding of teeth. (Matthew 24:46-53)*

I believe this kind of salt-filled faith that is anticipated by Christ in His disciples is essential in our churches today and in the days to come. This kind of faith is His love, the salty kind that heals wounds. Without this kind of love, housed in temples born again in Christ and full of His promised Holy Spirit, the fruit on the vine will begin to wither and grow weak and bitter. Hearts left to sit within their self-made walls of sin protecting old wounds or idols will not persevere.

> *Christ loved the church and gave Himself up for her, So that He might sanctify her, having cleansed her by the washing of water with the Word, That He might present the church to Himself in glorious splendor, without spot or wrinkle or any such things [that she might be holy and faultless]. (Ephesians 5:25-27)*

There is a Hebrew feast called the Feast of Trumpets, or *Yom Truah*, which begins the series of fall feasts and leads to the final pilgrimage Feast of the Lord, called the Feast of Sukkot. This last of the biblical feasts was a foreshadowing of the ultimate goal of every Christian, to be in His presence continually, free from our false securities, and filled with His Spirit. The Feast of Sukkot is the call for all God's people to give up all that distracts them from worshipping only Him—to come and spend a week in what is called a *sukka*, which seems to afford little or no shelter from wind, rain or sun. But God promised to meet His people Israel there during the week they dedicate to this feast. He promises us in the New Covenant so much more. We can be assured of our righteousness because of Christ. We have the confidence to enter His *sukkah* (His presence) here and to hold firmly to the hope that He is making a place for us to be with Him in heaven for all eternity (John 14:3).

In His Spirit, our spirit will be renewed until we love Him with our whole heart and find the supernatural ability to love others as He would love them. We walk this salvation path with fear and trembling (Philippians 2:12). He wants all of our heart, soul, and strength. It is a narrow and costly road to walk for us who have so much to give up. To become completely and utterly dependent on Him and Him alone for our security, peace, and understanding is a process that I believe will take us more than a lifetime to fully accomplish.

The Festival of Trumpets reminds us we don't have much longer to let Him begin this essential work in our hearts. The trumpet call of this feast represents His Spirit reminding us that we should be on our way. It is a warning call to those of us in the fields working His harvest that the great and ultimate day is drawing near. May we be found in Him working for His glory when that day comes.

> *Blow the trumpet in Zion; sound an alarm on My holy Mount [Zion]. Let all the inhabitants of the land tremble, for the day of [the judgment of] the Lord is coming; it is close at hand.* (Joel 2:1)

Truah[26] or *trumpet* is also the shout of triumph made by the best man at the Jewish wedding when the groom has received his bride to himself under the huppa. *Truah* sounds like a great shout of unity and confidence in the One who saves us! It is a shout of praise and thanksgiving

---

[26] The Complete Word Study: Old Testament, King James Version. Zodhiates, Spiros, Th.D.AMG Publishers Chattanooga, TN 37422, USA. 1994. P. 2365.#7321 *Rua* and P. 126. Hebrew and Chaldee Dictionary. #8643 *Trua*.

Completely His

that takes down walls of resistance and sends the enemy running. It is a shout of victory hoped for and believed in because He has done it, He is making a place for us, He is coming back for us and we have grown to completely trust Him.

> *So the people shouted, and the trumpets were blown. When the people heard the sound of the trumpet, they raised a great shout, and [Jericho's] wall fell down in its place, so that the [Israelites] went up into the city, every man straight before him, and they took the city.* (Joshua 6:20)

Joshua could have tried to take down the walls of Jericho his own way. He had the power to obey or not. We all have that choice every day in everything we do. When we seek God's will and He tells us the way, we obey by acting in faith and choosing to obey Him. This gives God the glory and deepens our joy. There was a man named Cornelius in the New Testament who had this character. Paul describes him as a man that asked God about everything and this was pleasing to God (Acts 10:1-2).

God's response to Cornelius' heart was to send a messenger to let him know that "Your prayers and your charities have come up as a memorial before God" (Acts 10:4b, ONM). A memorial is defined as a sweet smelling incense to God. Cornelius seemed to have a deep heart desire to draw nearer to God, so God drew near to him by sending Peter to see him. God did not need affirmation that Cornelius might accept Jesus. God knew he would, and He trusted Peter to carry out His plan, His way. Peter obeyed each part of the plan and, in the end, Cornelius alone didn't believe in what Peter taught him, Cornelius' whole household believed. Even before Peter could baptize them with water, God poured out His Spirit of truth and power on all of them! What an amazing moment!

Peter was "amazed because the gift of the Holy Spirit fell even upon the heathens: for they heard them speaking in tongues and glorifying God." Peter responded, "No one can deny the water, can they, for any of these to be immersed, who took the Holy Spirit like we did?" And he ordered them to be immersed in the name of Y'shua Messiah (Jesus our Messiah)" (Acts 10:45-48, ONM). Peter had obeyed God against all his own understanding and had gone into a heathen household to preach the Gospel. He trusted God's plan and did not call unclean what God had cleansed (Acts 10:9-34).

Perhaps a great *truah* was sounded in heaven that day for God's plan had begun to unfold, and the light would go to the Gentiles and to all the nations. A wall of division had come down when Jesus was resurrected and became the First Fruits for a great harvest of souls. Peter had faith that the wall of partition between Jew and Gentile was gone and he acted on that in faith and it produced glorious fruit for the kingdom of God.

> *But each in his own rank and turn: Christ (the Messiah) [is] the first fruits, then those who are Christ's [own will be resurrected] at His coming. After that comes the end (the completion), when He delivers over the kingdom to God the Father after rendering inoperative and abolishing every [other] rule and every authority and power. For [Christ] must be King and reign until He has put all [His] enemies under His feet. The last enemy to be subdued and abolished is death.* (1 Corinthians 15:23-26)

Jesus challenges us to extend to each other the same unconditional forgiveness we have been given through His death and resurrection on the cross. In Him we are challenged to let go of what is behind and press forward toward what lies ahead, the hope of our salvation.

> *Not that I have now attained [this ideal], or have already been made perfect, but I press on to lay hold of (grasp) and make my own, that for which Christ Jesus (the Messiah) has laid hold of me and made me His own. I do not consider, brethren, that I have captured and made it my own [yet]; but one thing I do [it is my one aspiration]: forgetting what lies behind and straining forward to what lies ahead,*

I press on toward the goal to win the [supreme and heavenly] prize to which God in Christ Jesus is calling us upward. (Phil 3:12-14)

When we can understand even a little bit of how much He loves us, we are changed. His heart and faithfulness, if we have allowed the wilderness to show us, encourages us that we are loved so deeply that we can risk a tender heart that seeks to keep intimacy with Jesus by confessing our sins and asking for the grace to go and sin no more. On the other hand, staying in our safe and familiar places will often mean our hearts go untested. This can mean that sin goes unrecognized or ignored. This kind of untested faith leaves us with hearts that resist or ignore conviction. A person needs to allow the Holy Spirit to develop a sensitivity in them that recognizes the conviction of sin and encourages them to repent. Then they must commit to walking out the process of breaking old habits of sin so that the healing and rebuilding of trust can take place. Sometimes there are still consequences for our sin, even after forgiveness has been given. This isn't always the case, but it is some of the time.

An insensitive heart resists any conviction because it has fear. Satan has a foot in the door of our hearts until we refuse to walk in fear. Fear is always based in deception. How does this deception get in and become a choice for us? A deliberate perversion of the truth is usually going to be rooted in the fear of losing something or someone that is important to us. We elect to live a lie in order to keep something we consider a treasure. Or, we lie in order to induce another person to do something or part with something that we desire for ourselves. Living a lie is living fraudulently. Jacob was being fraudulent when he tricked Esau into exchanging his birthright for lentil stew (Genesis 25:34). Abraham was being fraudulent when he convinced Sarah to lie about being his sister (Genesis 20:2). Saul was fraudulent when he tried to convince Samuel he hadn't done anything wrong by keeping some sheep (1 Samuel 15:14).

> *Woe to those who call evil good and good evil, who put darkness for light and light for darkness, who put bitter for sweet and sweet for bitter!* (Isaiah 5:20)

Eventually, God impresses on us what He shares in Ephesians 4, especially verses 23-25. We are to constantly seek to be renewed in the spirit of our mind, seeking the perspective of Jesus in all things. We are to seek this new perspective so that we can see how He sees us and our circumstances and, especially, how He sees our hearts. We are to believe what He sees and obey what He tells us to do. This will give us His nature in our hearts, His image replacing our own. He sees us holy as He is holy. We have the responsibility to allow Him to put that holiness to work on our character. That means separating ourselves from the old self and its habits and patterns, and clothing our hearts in the new that is Him. Therefore, we are to be about rejecting all that is fraudulent in our lives. We ask Him to change us so that we will only express the truth with those people He has in our lives. We have been put in our families, work places, and neighborhoods for a reason. He allows us to work out our salvation alongside of them with His Holy Spirit until His righteousness takes over our whole heart.

> *For My thoughts are not your thoughts, neither are your ways My ways, says the Lord. For as the heavens are higher than the earth, so are My ways higher than your ways and My thoughts than your thoughts.* (Isaiah 55:8-9)

The key is to run this race by God's plan, timing, and for His purposes. His purpose is that we would be glorifying Him by reflecting the love of God the Father, Jesus the Son and the Holy Spirit. As they are one, we are to be one. I believe that the trumpet has sounded its warning to the Church. I believe that God has spoken to the Church and that it is time to prepare our hearts for a new direction based on wisdom from the beginning. We must be a church that listens, hears and obeys His Word and worships Him in Spirit and truth.

> *You worship what you do not know; we know what we worship, for salvation is of the Jews. But the hour is coming, and now is, when the true worshipers will worship the Father in spirit and truth; for the Father is seeking such to worship Him. God is Spirit, and those who worship Him must worship in spirit and truth."* (John 4:22-24, NKJV).

Yom Kippur is the feast that follows *Yom Truah*. This is when the Jews were commanded to confess and repent for any sins they had committed over the year. The High Priest, only on this day, was invited to go into the Holy of Holies in the Tabernacle. On this day a sacrifice of blood, representing the sins of the nation would be made and it would be sprinkled over two goats, one that would be sacrificed on the altar and the other to be offered as a scapegoat. The scapegoat foreshadowed the Jewish hope for the coming Messiah. This goat sprinkled with the blood of the sacrifice was led into the wilderness with the sins of Israel carried on its back. When it did not return, the hope was that those sins had been forgiven.

When the Romans destroyed the temple in 67 AD, all of the sacrificial feasts ceased. Rabbinic Judaism developed its own laws and traditions to practice in the place of the temple sacrifices. They substituted this new system of laws for what Jesus had offered them as their Messiah. Substitutes are never good, and Rabbinic Judaism is really just a substitute. Jesus had become the perfect, once and for all sacrifice, meant to replace all sacrifices at the temple forever. In Him we can learn to be in His presence all the time, to walk with Him, talk with Him, and commune with Him every day, all day. What an incredible gift came to us through God's people, Israel. We have the power in Him to enter through the door of Christ to the Holy of Holies and be with Him all the time. Everyone is to have the opportunity to know Him this way, particularly our Jewish friends and neighbors and equally the Gentiles.

Following *Yom Kippur* is the Feast of Tabernacles, also called *Sukkot*. On the Hebrew calendar[27], *Sukkot* is the last of the pilgrimage feasts of the year and forshadowed the special promise of a coming Savior. Other names for this feast are Feast of Tabernacles or Feast of Booths. It is a time for the nation of Israel to gather together to worship the Lord in community, declaring to Him that He is their only source of security, hope and affection. This feast promised God's people that resting in His presence was available to them if they had followed His commandments at *Yom Truah* and *Yom Kippur*. If they had sincerely prepared themselves for Him and sought Him as their only source of security and help, He promised them His rest at *Sukkot*.

> *Therefore the Lord Himself shall give you a sign: Behold, the young woman who is unmarried and a virgin shall conceive and bear a son, and shall call his name Immanuel [God with us].* (Isaiah 7:14)

Traditionally, this would have been the time to celebrate the fall harvest, with the presentation of the third first fruits of the growing season. All the "first fruit" offerings were commanded of Israel once they entered the Promised Land (Deuteronomy 26). They were presented by Israel to the priests at the temple for approval and then left with them as a sort of tithe offering. This was the means by which the Levites were provided for by God.

The first fruit offering to the priests at the temple would have been at the time of the spring harvest at Passover. This was the fruit of the barley harvest and it foreshadowed Jesus who is our first fruits.

> *For just as [because of their union of nature] in Adam all people die, so also [by virtue of their union of nature] shall all in Christ be made alive. But each in his own rank and turn: Christ (the Messiah) [is] the firstfruits, then those who are Christ's [own will be resurrected]*

---

[27] Our favorite source for Hebrew Heritage calendars is shared with you on acknowledgment page.

> *at His coming. After that comes the end (the completion), when He delivers over the kingdom to God the Father after rendering inoperative and abolishing every [other] rule and every authority and power. For [Christ] must be King and reign until He has put all [His] enemies under His feet. The last enemy to be subdued and abolished is death.* (1 Corinthians 15:22-26).

The latter fruits, or second first fruits, would traditionally have been the bread loaves made with the wheat of the late harvest and presented at Pentecost (also called *Shavuot*) and baked with the new leaven for the year. This offering foreshadowed those who are Christ's own, made new in Him. The third first fruits, offered up at *Sukkot*, is the completion of the entire growing season.

A true fulfillment of *Sukkot* in the heart of His Church, in us, our family and all those He has called is the hope of entering His rest. To reach this hope we press forward in faith.

> *And the city has no need of the sun nor of the moon to give light to it, for the splendor and radiance (glory) of God illuminate it, and the Lamb is its lamp. The nations shall walk by its light and the rulers and leaders of the earth shall bring into it their glory. And its gates shall never be closed by day, and there shall be no night there. They shall bring the glory (the splendor and majesty) and the honor of the nations into it. But nothing that defiles or profanes or is unwashed shall ever enter it, nor anyone who commits abominations (unclean, detestable, morally repugnant things) or practices falsehood, but only those whose names are recorded in the Lamb's Book of Life.* (Revelation 21:23-27).

There are two traditions in the Feast of Tabernacles or *Sukkot* that also foreshadow our coming Savior. One was a ceremony where a rabbi would draw water from the pool of Siloam, pour the water from that pool at the foot of the altar into silver basins and Jews would pray to

God for rain to soften their fields for the next season of planting (it was the rainy season). The second tradition was to pray to God for a Messiah who would bring God's salvation to Israel. Typically, Isaiah 12:3 is recited as the water is poured. *"With joy you will draw from the wells of salvation."* The gold of the altar is the symbol of deity and the silver of the basins is the symbol of redemption of man; Jesus pouring forth into man His Holy Spirit (water) in continuance from the river of water that ever flows from the Temple of God. When we are in Him, we are to be built up in Him as His temple. The water of His Spirit is to be what others and we draw from for healing life.

> *Now on the final and most important day of the Feast, Jesus stood, and He cried in a loud voice, If any man is thirsty, let him come to Me and drink! He who believes in Me [who cleaves to and trusts in and relies on Me] as the Scripture has said, From his innermost being shall flow [continuously] springs and rivers of living water.* (John 7:37-38)

Verses 37 and 38 are talking about two different forms of water, both from the same living source, who is Jesus. He was telling His people that they were invited to drink from Him and that if they would believe and come to totally rely on Him, the same living water would flow from them and out to others. The words "Out of his belly, as the scripture has said, shall flow springs and rivers of living water," refers to Scripture as a whole that points to Jesus, as our only source for living water.

> *And if you pour out that with which you sustain your own life for the hungry and satisfy the need of the afflicted, then shall your light rise in darkness, and your obscurity and gloom become like the noonday. And the Lord shall guide you continually and satisfy you in drought and in dry places and make strong your bones. And you shall be like a watered garden and like a spring of water whose waters fail not. And your ancient ruins shall be rebuilt; you shall raise up the foundations of [buildings that have laid waste for] many generations;*

> *and you shall be called Repairer of the Breach, Restorer of Streets to Dwell In.* (Isaiah 58:10-12)

Jesus compares Himself to the river of waters issuing from beneath the temple. We are to allow ourselves to be built up into His temple that houses His precious Spirit within us and from whom we learn to drink continually, drawing more and more and deeper and deeper into who we are in Him. When the winds of persecution and affliction blow, He can lead the thirsty to our wells, and we can offer them living water to drink.

> *Therefore with joy will you draw water from the wells of salvation.* (Isaiah 12:3)

Sukkot is an invitation from God to spend time drawing from His well and resting in His presence, celebrating His provision. Traditionally, each family builds a *sukkah*, or booth, outside their home. This is a flimsy structure of palm branches that provides shade, but not much else (picture Jonah's weed). In our own eyes and understanding it seems obvious that a good rain or strong wind will blow that cover right off and those inside will get wet and messy. Rain can soak through the walls and the ground can become saturated. The family who chooses to celebrate *Sukkot* traditionally eats all of the week's meals outside in the *sukkah*, and the men are supposed to sleep in it. It is to be a room for visitors, even strangers, to come in and share stories and meals.

For those who have received Christ, we are invited to a *sukkah* that is far better than the one offered in the Old Testament. The invitation to the Jews was contingent on their being right in the eyes of God, cleansed from sin and all unrighteousness. There is only one way that we have that guarantee and it is through our Savior Jesus Christ. Many are called, but few are chosen.

The heart of His people cried out for a deliverer from Egypt and He heard their cry and sent Moses. For thousands of years they prayed for a Messiah to save them from oppression and He heard their cry. In His mercy He granted them His salvation through Christ. Will we receive what His hand is so lovingly offering to us? Or will we test Him as they tested Him in the wilderness. Will the giants overwhelm our trust and keep us from His heart that is our only hope of love.

> *Take care, brothers and sisters, that there not be in any one of you a wicked, unbelieving heart [which refuses to trust and rely on the Lord, a heart] that turns away from the living God. But continually encourage one another every day, as long as it is called "Today" [and there is an opportunity], so that none of you will be hardened [into settled rebellion] by the deceitfulness of sin [its cleverness, delusive glamour, and sophistication]. For we [believers] have become partakers of Christ [sharing in all that the Messiah has for us], if only we hold firm our newborn confidence [which originally led us to Him] until the end, while it is said,*
>
> *"Today [while there is still opportunity] if you hear His voice, Do not harden your heart, as when they provoked Me [in the rebellion in the desert at Meribah]." (Hebrews 3:12-15)*

In Him we can learn to enter the perfect *sukkah* of His love. In His rest we will find strength and protection through any storm, no matter how severe. In Christ, our roof has become our God. In Christ our path is lit only by His Light. Our tongues are salted by His Word and we drink deeply of the water of life that is Jesus.

> *And the Word (Christ) became flesh (human, incarnate) and tabernacled (fixed His tent of flesh, lived awhile) among us; and we [actually] saw His glory (His honor, His majesty), such glory as an only begotten son receives from his father, full of grace (favor, lovingkindness) and truth. (John 1:14)*

Our family was able to *sukkah* together one last time before our precious son-in-law was deployed on the USS Makin Island for a tour of the south Pacific. We gathered in the tent we call home in Plymouth, Minnesota and prayed, talked, hugged, and rested. Sitting shoulder to shoulder with my sweet daughter and her husband, I listened as she confided her dreams and theirs for the future they are planning to have together once he is home.

A few short weeks after our visit, she stood on the cement platform in front of the boat that would carry her bridegroom far away from her sight. Their faith, grounded in Christ and built firmly on His faithfulness, is fully trustworthy.

Jesus is our rock and sure foundation. In Him we move and have our being. In Him we will walk out this wilderness as we allow Him to prepare our hearts for whatever lies ahead.

As the disciples stood and watched Jesus be lifted up into the clouds, far away from their sight, so we also stand, with our hearts longing for Him. When we lose our lives for Christ, we lose it all so that we may serve Him.

We know what that means, we count the cost, and with our eyes fixed on Him, we go.

> The Lord bless you and keep you; the Lord make His face to shine upon you and be gracious to you; the Lord lift up His countenance upon you and give you peace
>
> Y'va-re-kh'cha A-do-nai v'yeesh'm'recha;
> Ya-eir A-do-nai pa-nav ei-ley-cha vee-chun-nei-cha;
> Yee-sa A-do-nai pa-nav ei-lay-cha v'ya-sem l'cha sha-lom
> Amen